Remembering Christ at Christmas

Remembering Christ at Christmas

Monte F. Shelley

S△P
Summit View Publishing
Orem, Utah

Front cover art: *Birth of Jesus* © Del Parson. Used by permission.
Cover design by Jacob Rawlins

© 2008 Monte F. Shelley

All rights reserved. No part of this book may be reproduced in any form or by any means without written permission from the author.

Summit View Publishing
Orem, Utah 84097
www.SummitViewPublishing.com

Library of Congress Control Number: 2008906152
ISBN-13: 978-0-9818692-5-4
ISBN-10: 0-9818692-5-4

Printed in the United States of America
First printing: August 2008
10 9 8 7 6 5 4 3 2 1

CONTENTS

PREFACE v
ACKNOWLEDGEMENTS vii
LIST OF ABBREVIATIONS viii
1 SEEING CHRIST IN CHRISTMAS TRADITIONS 1
   Xmas 6
   Santa Claus 6
   Santa's Elves 8
   Rudolph, the Red Nosed Reindeer 8
   Christmas Tree 8
   Other Christmas Traditions 15
   Giving and Receiving Gifts 19
2 NATIVITY STORIES 27
   On What Day Was Jesus Born? 29
   In What Year Was Jesus Born? 30
   Where Was Jesus Born? 32
   No Room in the Inn 34
   Caravansary or Khan 36
   Kataluma 38
   Birth of Jesus 43
   Shepherds Watching Their Flock 48
   Name and Blessing 52
   Temple Offering 52
   Wise Men 53
   Which of the Stories Is Correct? 59
3 ADVENT TREES AND CALENDARS 63
   Nature Ornaments 66
   Constellation Ornaments 97
   Conclusion 122
4 HAVE A "MARY" CHRISTMAS 123
APPENDIX: MADAME LYDIA MOUNTFORD 129
BIBLIOGRAPHY 133
   A. Books and Articles 133
   B. Illustrations 140

PREFACE

In December 2006, I was invited to give a Christmas lesson in a church meeting. I decided to focus on how we can remember Christ during the Christmas season.

A common way to remember Christ at Christmas is to remember the first Christmas. In our family, we set up a small nativity scene and display some paintings of the nativity. We see nativity scenes as we visit homes, businesses, churches, and Temple Square. We see Christmas programs or plays at church. On Christmas Eve, we read Luke's account and the Book of Mormon account of the first Christmas.

For the lesson, I decided to share several different versions of the nativity story. As I prepared the lesson, I found other versions of the story that were quite interesting and different from the familiar nativity story. These stories are based on different interpretations of the scriptural accounts and on different understandings of linguistic and historical evidence from oral traditions, ancient manuscripts, Jewish traditions, and archaeology. These stories helped me better understand and appreciate the nativity story. As Elder Bruce R. McConkie said, "unless or until some of the saints ... see in a dream or a vision the inn where Joseph and Mary and Jesus spent that awesome night, we can only *speculate* as to the details" (McConkie, I:344; italics added). In the lesson, I also wanted to share some of the ways I had learned to use common Christmas traditions and symbols as mnemonics (memory helps) to remind me of Christ and the true meaning of Christmas. This allowed me to learn and share some fascinating things about the language of scriptural symbolism as it relates to the symbolism of Christmas traditions.

I prepared a PowerPoint presentation with pictures to illustrate the ideas. After I gave the presentation, quite a few people asked for copies to share with their families. Later I shared the same lesson with my adult children and their families. They also wanted copies. I decided to prepare an extended version that I could share with family and friends. During this process, I found more information that has helped me better understand the nativity and the language of symbolism.

Last summer I attended two BYU Education Week classes by Donna B. Nielsen. She talked about some oral traditions of Christian peasants in Palestine that she shares in her audio CD called *Holy Child Jesus*. I have included some of these oral traditions that relate to the nativity. Donna also talked about advent trees or calendars. My wife reminded me that we used advent calendars when our children were small. I have added some ideas for advent trees based on common outdoor nature symbols that can remind us of Christ at Christmas and throughout the year. This allowed me to share more about the language of scriptural symbolism with my family and friends. As we observe, reflect on, and more fully appreciate the wonders of nature, we can share scriptural events and symbolism that help us remember Christ at Christmas and throughout the year.

ACKNOWLEDGEMENTS

I am grateful for my wife, Elona, who spent many hours editing and taking pictures, and for my children, and their families who helped in the preparation of this book. I appreciate Terrence L. Szink, Andrew C. Skinner, Donna B. Nielsen, S. Kent Brown, Norman Shelley and Leanne Shelley for their feedback on early drafts. Special thanks go to Kelley Konzak for editing and to Jacob Rawlins for the cover design.

I appreciate those who granted me permission to use their images to illustrate many of the ideas in this book. I believe pictures can help us imagine and understand much faster than words do. I have included images of some of my favorite paintings by Joseph Brickey, Simon Dewey, Derek Hegsted, Del Parson, and Liz Lemon Swindle. I have also included images and photos from D. Kelly Ogden, John Pratt, and others. Section B of the bibliography provides information about the images, sources, copyrights, and where to find the images.

At www.SummitViewPublishing.com you will find: (a) links to websites where you can see color prints, (b) links to online articles, (c) a link to the book distributor, (d) information about where the book is available in stores and online, and (e) information about other publications. You will also be able to submit comments or suggestions.

LIST OF ABBREVIATIONS

The following abbreviations are used in the text, footnotes and bibliography.

ANF   Roberts, Alexander and James Donaldson, eds., *The Anti-Nicene Fathers*, (10 vols., 1885–96: Christian Literature Publishing Company).

BAG   Walter Bauer, William F. Arndt and F. Wilbur Gingrich. *A Greek-English Lexicon of the New Testament*, 2d ed. (1979: University of Chicago Press).

BD   *Bible Dictionary.* (1981: The Church of Jesus Christ of Latter-day Saints).

BDB   Brown, F., S. Driver, and C. Briggs, *The Brown-Driver-Briggs Hebrew and English Lexicon*, (c1906, 1996: Hendrickson Publishers).

DBI   *Dictionary of Biblical Imagery*, edited by Leland Ryken, James C. Wilhoit, Temper Longman III (1998: InterVarsity Press Academic).

GR   Greek word means

GTS   *Guide to the Scriptures.* In the *The Scriptures: CD-ROM Edition 1.1.* (2001: The Church of Jesus Christ of Latter-day Saints).

HC   *History of the Church.* (1949: The Church of Jesus Christ of Latter-day Saints).

HEB   Hebrew word means

Hymns	*Hymns of The Church of Jesus Christ of Latter-day Saints*. (1985: The Church of Jesus Christ of Latter-day Saints).
JST	*Joseph Smith Translation* of the Bible
KJV	*King James Version* of the Bible
LTJC	Holzapfel, Richard Neitzel and Thomas A. Wayment, *The Life and Teachings of Jesus Christ*, (2003–2006: Deseret Book) 3 volumes.
NIV	*New International Version* of the Bible.
OTSM	*Old Testament Student Manual Genesis–2 Samuel*. (1980–1981: The Church of Jesus Christ of Latter-day Saints).
RSV	*Revised Standard Version* of the Bible
SOED	*The Shorter Oxford English Dictionary*, (1973: Oxford University Press).
TDOT	*Theological Dictionary of the Old Testament*, edited by G. Johannes Botterweck, Helmer Ringgren, Heinz-Josef Fabry, vol. 1–15, (1974–2006: Eerdmans).
TPJS	*Teachings of the Prophet Joseph Smith*, compiled by Joseph Fielding Smith, (1976: Deseret Book or 2002: Covenant Communications, Inc.).

For scripture references, the abbreviations are found in *The Scriptures* published by The Church of Jesus Christ of Latter-day Saints. *The Scriptures* includes the King James Version of the Bible, Book of Mormon, Doctrine and Covenants, and the Pearl of Great Price. Unless otherwise noted, all Bible quotations come from the King James Version. Italics in scripture quotations have been added.

1

SEEING CHRIST
IN CHRISTMAS TRADITIONS

Years ago, I saw a picture that can be seen as either a vase or two faces looking at each other. Later, 3-D images became popular.

2-D Rubin's goblet-profile[1]   *3-D Teapot* © Hidetomo Katsura

Although a 3-D picture doesn't change, where you *focus* your eyes determines what you *see*. Some people only see a strange pattern while others see a 3-D image. What you *see* determines how you *feel* and how you respond. Some people *love* these pictures because they can see a 3-D image. Others *hate* them because they have tried many times but have not been able to see a 3-D image. After a 30 second "eye exam," I have helped over 100 of these people see a 3-D image within about five minutes. I enjoy seeing how their feelings change from frustration to excitement when they see it the first time.

---

[1] "Rubin's Goblet-Profile" (*Stereogram*, Candace Books: 1994, p. 15) is a 3-D version of the vase-face illusion.

Epictetus, a Greek philosopher said, "We are disturbed not by what happens to us, but by our thoughts about what happens to us" (Katie, viii). People are disturbed not by looking at a 3-D picture like the one above but by their thoughts about it (e.g., why can't I see a 3-D image like everyone else?).

Some people are disturbed not by the *Christus* statue but by their thoughts about it. They see a "graven image" expressly forbidden by the Ten Commandments (Ex. 20:4). Other people see a reminder of the glory and love of the Savior, but they do not worship the statue.

Likewise, some people are disturbed not by Christmas traditions but by their thoughts about the traditions. They feel "Xmas" takes Christ out of Christmas and that "holiday" has lost the meaning of "holy day." They are offended to hear "Happy Holidays" instead of "Merry Christmas" in stores. They see commercialism, pagan traditions, Christmas trees and decorations, Santa Claus, elves, and reindeer.

One college professor gives an annual "anti-Claus" lecture because he feels Santa hides the real meaning of Christmas. He says, "Santa Claus has become the central figure in the commercialization of Christmas," parents lie when they say Santa is real, and "the letters of Santa can be rearranged to spell Satan" (Speckman).

Other people see Christmas traditions as pagan practices. Early Christians began celebrating Christmas on December 25th when the pagan sun god was worshipped. During that pagan festival, people decked the halls with holly and evergreen wreaths, exchanged gifts, and had lavish feasts. Some early Americans were disturbed by these pagan traditions. "To the New England Puritans, Christmas was sacred. The pilgrims' second governor, William Bradford, wrote that he tried hard to stamp out 'pagan mockery' of the observance, penalizing any frivolity. The influential Oliver Cromwell preached against 'the heathen traditions' of Christmas carols, decorated trees, and any joyful expression that desecrated 'that sacred event' " (http://www.history.com; search for *Cromwell Christmas tree*).

Stone pillars at Gezer © Todd Bolen

Long before Moses, pagans set up stone pillars to honor their gods or remember important events. However, God told Joshua to set up twelve stones to help future Israelites remember that God cut off the waters of the river Jordan so Joshua and their fathers could cross on dry ground into the promised land (Josh. 4). Likewise,

Jacob set up a stone after his dream at Bethel (Gen. 28:18–28), Moses set up twelve stone pillars after receiving the Ten Commandments (Ex. 24:2–4), and Joshua set up a stone after renewing the covenant at Shechem (Josh. 24:27). Ironically, the Lord and his prophets used this pagan practice to help future generations remember what God did. However, the Lord hated stone pillars used for idol worship (Deut. 16:22; 12:3).

Moses and the Brass Serpent by Judith Mehr © Intellectual Reserve, Inc.

When the Israelites were bitten by poisonous serpents, the Lord commanded Moses to lift up a brass serpent on a pole to heal people who looked at it. This was a type or prophecy of the Messiah, who would be lifted up that all who looked on him with faith might have eternal life (Hel. 8:13–15). Centuries later, "the brasen serpent that Moses had made" was destroyed because the people worshipped it instead of God (2 Kgs. 18:4).

Some people are disturbed by the pagan origins of Christmas and Easter. "But it seems that the critical thing is not what their origins are, but whether we are worshipping the one true God. ... [Do] these holidays glorify God like the standing stones by the Jordan did ... [by being] a continual reminder of the wonderful thing God has done by sending the promised Messiah" (Tverberg 2004a)?

Clearly it is possible to look at Christmas traditions without seeing Christ and be disturbed. However, it is also possible to change our focus so we can see Christ in *Christ*mas traditions even if others do not.

Parables and temple teachings use obvious words and symbols both to reveal and to conceal messages. Parables are short stories that *link* an ordinary object (e.g., a mustard seed) or event (e.g., the lost sheep) with a spiritual truth. Often the disciples had to ask Jesus for the meaning of a parable. From then on, the familiar story or object reminded disciples of the new meaning now linked to it. If we *link* Christ-related meanings to familiar Christmas traditions, they will help us "always remember" Christ (D&C 20:79). Humor, Exaggeration, and Action strengthen the Links and HEAL our memory. Thus, even fantasy can become a mnemonic to help us remember what we link to it.

On the following pages are some memory links that can help us remember or see Christ in Christmas traditions.

Xmas

The Greek word for Christ is Χριστος, or *christos*. The first letter is "chi." In an ancient Greek New Testament manuscript[2] written in all capital letters, Christ (ΧΡΙΣΤΟΣ) was abbreviated as ΧΣ, ΧΝ, ΧΥ, ΧΕ, or ΧΩ. The first letter, "chi," represented Christ, and the second letter was the last letter of the word, which indicated how the word *Christ* was used in the sentence (e.g., subject, object, indirect object). About AD 315, Constantine used the first two letters, ΧΡ (chi-rho), as a symbol on his flag.

In the 1500s, typesetting was done by hand. To save costs, the church used Χ (chi) for "Christ." Xmas, Xian and Xianity became common abbreviations. Similarly, in our time, using a phone to type a text message is tedious and has resulted in many abbreviations like BRB (be right back) and BTW (by the way). Pronouncing Xmas as "chi-mas" or Christmas will help us see Christ in *X*mas.

Santa Claus

Santa reminds some people of Satan and others of the Christlike Saint Nicholas who loved children and used his inheritance to help the needy. Others focus on interesting similarities between Santa and Christ. The following is a list of some of these similarities.

---

[2] See Matt. 26:68; Eph. 1:1; 3:17, and 4:15 in Vercellone, *Biblionum Sacrorum Graecus Codex Vaticanus*. Note: Each abbreviation has a line over the two letters. In the old script ΧΣ and ΧΩ were written as ΧC and Χω respectively. Other similar abbreviations were used for Jesus (IY), Lord (KY), and God (ΘY) as seen in Eph.1:1–2.

1. Santa dresses in red (atonement) and white (purity). When Christ comes again, he "shall be red in his apparel" (D&C 133:48–51; Isa. 63:2; Rev. 19:13).
2. "The hair of his head was white like the pure snow" (D&C 110:3; Rev. 1:14).
3. He ascends into and descends from heaven (Acts 1:9–10; 1 Thes. 4:16; 3 Ne. 11:8; 18:39).
4. His sleigh pulled by flying reindeer reminds us of (a) the "chariot of fire and horses of fire" that took Elijah into heaven (2 Kgs. 2:11) and (b) the chariot throne of God, pulled by cherubim depicted as animals with wings, symbolizing the ability to move quickly on earth and in heaven (Ezek. 10; D&C 77:4).
5. His coming is in the night "as a thief" who enters not by the door (D&C 106:4; 1 Thes. 5:2; John 10:1; 20:19).
6. He is happy, loving, and giving.
7. He invites little children to come unto him (3 Ne. 17:11, 21; Matt. 19:14).
8. Little children believe in him.
9. We are invited to become as little children.
10. He knows if you've been bad or good.
11. He rewards every person according to his works.
12. Gifts are given personally and anonymously.

13. We ask for gifts or blessings.
14. We don't get everything we ask for.
15. Santa gives children unearned gifts that they cannot get without him. Christ offers us the unearned gifts of immortality and eternal life.
16. We are not always grateful for the gifts we receive.

Santa Claus also reminds us of the four stages of life:
1. You believe in Santa.
2. You don't believe in Santa.
3. You are Santa.
4. You look like Santa.

Santa's Elves

Santa's elves are "subordinate clauses" who help Santa accomplish his mission. Christ also has helpers called angels, prophets, Church leaders, priesthood holders, Relief Society members, missionaries, and other disciples to help him "bring to pass ... the eternal life of man" (Moses 1:39) which is the "greatest of all the gifts of God" (D&C 14:7).

Rudolph, the Red Nosed Reindeer

Rudolph was a guide like Christ. He too was "despised and rejected" by his peers (Isa. 53:3). Only he could save them. When there was fog ("mist of darkness"), he was the "light which shineth in darkness" (D&C 6:21) and others followed.

Christmas Tree

Paradise Tree: In Germany during the middle ages, a popular outdoor religious play about Adam and Eve was held on December 24th. An evergreen tree represented the

Tree of Life because it never loses its color or needles. It is also a sign of the hope that new life will return in the spring. The paradise tree was adorned with red apples. The play ended with the promise that a savior would be born (*The New Encyclopedia Britannica*, 15th ed., s.v. "Christmas tree"; *The World Book Encyclopedia*, 2002, s.v. "Christmas").

The **Tree of Life** in the Garden of Eden represents eternal life and God's presence. It is found in the art and writings of every Mediterranean culture before and after Lehi left that area. Different cultures believed the Tree of Life was a white cypress tree, a date palm tree, an evergreen tree (arborvitae), or an olive tree (Griggs 1988, 27–29). Some olive trees are over a thousand years old.

Tree of Life © Derek Hegsted

The **fruit** of the Tree of Life in Lehi's Dream was white, sweet, and desirable to make one happy (1 Ne. 8:10). The tree represented the love of God as expressed through the ministry and atonement of Christ (1 Ne. 11:21–33). The fruit of the tree was the "greatest of all the gifts of God" (1 Ne. 15:36) which is eternal life (D&C 14:7).

From *Lehi's Dream* by Jerry Thompson © Intellectual Reserve, Inc.

The **olive tree** was the Tree of Life according to Jewish tradition. It provides food, light, heat, lumber, ointments, and medicine. It is ever-bearing and always green. If it is chopped down, life will spring from its roots suggesting everlasting life and resurrection. "Olive oil … was not only used … for the ritual anointing of priests and kings, but was also used … for anointing the sick for God's blessing. (See Ex. 30:23–33; James 5:14–15.) The names *Christ* (Greek) and *Messiah* (Hebrew) both mean 'the anointed one' " (Griggs 2003, 763).

Olive Tree in Gethsemane © D. Kelly Ogden

Atonement: After the Last Supper, Jesus went to the Garden of Gethsemane on the slope of the Mount of Olives. Jesus "kneeled down, and prayed, Saying, Father, if thou be willing, remove this cup from me: nevertheless not my will, but thine, be done" (Luke 22:40).

Jesus Praying in Gethsemane by Harry Anderson © Intellectual Reserve, Inc

In Aramaic, Gethsemane means "olive press," a device that was used to press the oil out of olives. In Gethsemane Jesus fell to the ground, was strengthened by an angel, sweat blood from every pore as if being crushed like olives in a press, and trembled because of pain "so great [was] his anguish for the wickedness and the abominations of his people" (Luke 22:42–44; ; Matt. 26:39; Mark 14:35; Mos. 3:7; D&C 19:18). In the spirit world, "an innumerable company" of the righteous dead "were filled with joy and gladness, and were rejoicing together because the day of their deliverance was at hand." When Jesus visited them in the spirit world while his body was in the grave, "the saints rejoiced in their redemption, and bowed the knee and acknowledged the Son of God as their Redeemer and Deliverer from death and the chains of hell" (D&C 138:11–23).

The painting below shows the unidentified angel kneeling reverently beside Christ, strengthening him (Luke 22:43). "The angel seems to be saying these encouraging words, 'Well done Jehovah. Well done.' The joy and gratitude that may have been in the eyes of the angel might easily be overlooked" (Hegsted 2008).

Angel at Gethsemane © Derek J. Hegsted

Temple: "The tree of life in nearly every culture was either in the temple or took the place of the temple when the temple was absent" (Miller, 96). A menorah or candlestick with seven lamps was in the Holy Place (Terrestrial Room) before the veil of the Jerusalem temple. The menorah symbolized the tree of life (Griggs 1988, 28). It used olive oil as the fuel to provide light in the room. According to Jewish tradition, the seven lamps represent the seven periods of creation.

Herod's Temple, photo by Deror Avi

Cross: "The New Testament also alludes to the cross of Jesus as a tree. (See Acts 5:30; Gal. 3:13; 1 Pet. 2:24.) ... Some early Christians thought of the cross as a tree of life" (Griggs 1988, 30). The cross reminds some people of the crucifixion. Others see an *empty* cross that reminds them of the resurrection, as does the empty tomb.

An ancient Phoenician letter (X or †) was the origin of the Greek letter *tau* (Tτ) and the Hebrew letter *taw* or *tav* (ת). The name of this Hebrew letter, *taw* or *tav* (תָּו), means "mark" (Ezek. 9:4). Because this letter was anciently written as X or †, Xmas reminds some of the empty cross and the tree of life.

Christ: "Early Christians … likened the Savior to the tree of life. … His love and influence is over all, he is found in the temple, he is the 'Way' which leads to eternal life. He is the foundation of the world, the firstfruits of the resurrection. He offers healing power to the souls of all who will believe in him" (Miller, 94, 106).

Faith is like a seed. If we "*plant* this *word* [belief in Christ and his atonement] in [our] hearts, and … *nourish* it by [our] faith … it will become a *tree*, springing up in [us] unto *everlasting life*" (Alma 33:22–23).

Christmas trees remind us of (a) the Tree of Life in the Garden of Eden and in Lehi's dream, (b) the temple, (c) the empty cross, and (d) Christ's atonement, which makes eternal life possible. Like a steeple, they point heavenward. "To me the evergreens of Christmas are tokens of the hope that life and fragrance and beauty can survive the hostile  surrounds of winter. Christ is the true author of eternal life. Through him, we too can survive life's storms and freezes with dignity and vitality. Though planted in a sometimes hostile environment, we too can be evergreen" (Broderick, 101–102).

The star reminds us of the "star in the east" and the star of Bethlehem. The Nephites saw a "new star" as a sign of the birth of Jesus (Hel. 14:5; 3 Ne. 1:21). The star is "a symbol of Jesus, who is called the 'star out of Jacob' (Num. 24:17), and 'the bright and morning star' (Rev. 22:16)" (McConkie and Parry, 164). When the wise men saw the star, they came to Jerusalem and said, "Where is he that is born King of the Jews? for we have seen his *star in the east*, and are come to worship him" (Matt. 2:2). The star can remind us to "Come unto [Christ] and ye shall partake of the fruit of the tree of life" (Alma 5:34).

Ornaments and lights symbolize the fruit of the Tree of Life and the beauty of eternal life. Lights can remind us of (a) the white fruit on the tree in Lehi's dream, (b) the stars above Bethlehem on the night Jesus was born, and (c) the Light of Christ. Lights were originally candles meant to symbolize Christ, the Light of the World. Candles provide light and warmth by consuming their own substance, the wax. Christ gave his life that we might have eternal life.

Other Christmas Traditions

Christmas stockings symbolize the path we walk in life. If we follow the path that leads to the Tree of Life, we will receive the gift of eternal life that Christ has offered to all who are willing to receive it.

Candy canes symbolize shepherds' crooks used to protect sheep from predators and to bring lambs back to the fold. They remind us of the Good Shepherd who leaves the ninety and nine to rescue the one. Candy canes also remind us of the shepherds who saw the Lamb of God in a manger and shared what they had seen and heard.

Decorated homes honor Christ. *Outside* decorations "show that we are a 'light unto the world.' " *Inside* decorations "show that the love of Christ and his atonement is within" (Satterfield). "Let your light so shine ..., that they may see your good works and glorify your Father who is in heaven" (3 Ne. 12:16).

Wreaths are "round and green with red berries. This symbolizes that eternal life is everlasting [green circle] and brought about by the atonement [red]. In ancient Rome, a wreath was worn as a sign of victory. We celebrate Christ's victory in the Garden and on the Cross" (Satterfield).

Christmas ads remind us that Christmas is coming and to prepare early before the best gifts are gone and the stores close. Long before Christ was born, prophets prophesied of his birth. Early Christmas ads might remind us of prophecies that Christ is coming again and that we should prepare *now* like the five wise virgins did and not wait like the five foolish virgins (Matt. 25:1–13).

Shopping in crowded malls can remind us of the *first Christmas*. *Crowds* must have flocked into Bethlehem some 2,000 years ago when there was no room in the inn. *Packages* bring to mind the gifts brought to Christ by the wise men and of God's gift to us. *Music* that fills the malls brings images of the angelic choir that sang praises to God as the shepherds watched. *Excited children*, gazing at displays and decorations, remind us of the excited shepherds who told others what they had seen and heard. "Commercialism seems unimportant as my mind drifts back to that first Christmas" (Barney; quoting John A. Tvedtnes).

Shopping in crowded malls can also remind us of the *second coming*. *All* mankind should be "anxiously engaged in a good cause" such as bringing others the gift of eternal life. Only by serving others can we receive the gift Christ has given. All are invited to get ready for the second coming of Christ (Satterfield).

Christmas Eve: For Jews, a new day starts at sunset instead of at midnight. For them, Christmas Eve is the start of Christmas day. Jesus was born at night while shepherds watched over their flocks. Each Passover eve, Jewish families have a Seder meal to remember how Jehovah used the blood of lambs in delivering Israel, His *firstborn* son (Ex. 4:22), from Egypt. Jehovah (*firstborn*, lamb of God, and deliverer) may have been born on a Passover night (Pratt 1994, 38–45) while Jews left their doors open for Elijah (*Jehovah is my God*) during their Passover meal.

Christmas Morning symbolizes the second coming of Christ that marks the beginning of the millennium. On Christmas morning, everyone arises early to receive their gifts. On the morning of the first resurrection, we will rise to receive the gift of eternal life. Christmas day is a day of rest, rejoicing, and being with family and friends. A "White Christmas" reminds us of the purity that will exist during the Millennium (Satterfield).

Christmas Morning

Mistletoe is an evergreen plant with green leaves and white berries. Green symbolizes life and white, purity. The white berries can remind us of the fruit of the tree of life which was white and

"desirable to make one happy" (1 Ne. 8:10–11; Alma 32:41–42). The custom of kissing under the mistletoe can remind us that "the tree of life was a representation of the love of God" (1 Ne. 11:25) and that Christ said "all men [shall] know ye are my disciples, if ye have love one to another" (John 13:35). We are nothing if we have not charity, which is "the pure love of Christ" (Moro. 7:47).

More Traditions: Satterfield and Adamson also have suggestions regarding Frosty the Snowman, The Nutcracker, Christmas cards, Christmas tree stands, colors, bows, and bells.

Giving and Receiving Gifts

Gifts *from* God: "As Moses lifted up the serpent in the wilderness, even so must the Son of man be lifted up... For God so loved the world, that he gave his only begotten Son" (John 3:14, 16). Jesus Christ "so loved the world that he gave his own life, that as many as would believe might become the sons of God" (D&C 34:3) and receive the gift of everlasting life.

Golgotha © Derek J. Hegsted

"Christmas means giving. The Father gave his Son, and the Son gave his life. Without giving there is no true Christmas" (Hinckley 1983, 3). God has given us *life* through our parents; *love* from Him and for others; *peace* in adversity; and *eternal life* through the atonement (Monson, 6). God has also commanded us to seek earnestly the gifts of the Spirit (D&C 46:8).

The restoration of the gospel is another gift from God. When God wants to change the world, he sends a child. Joseph Smith was born December 23rd, two days after the shortest day of the year and two days before Christmas. Thus, the restoration began with the birth of Joseph as daylight hours began to increase on the earth. The restoration is part of the preparation for the second coming of the Savior that we can see in several Christmas traditions.

American Prophet © Del Parson

Gifts *to* God: What can we give to God?
- *Gifts to others* are gifts to God whether they cost us our money or time. Jewish teachings about beautifying God's commands and doing acts of loving kindness can help us celebrate Christmas by being more Christlike (Tverberg 2004b). These teachings are reflected in the hymn that says, "Have I done any good in the world today?" (*Hymns*, 223). We can give gifts of loving kindness. We can help the sick and the needy. We can lighten the burdens of others. We can be helpful, friendly, courteous, and kind. We can "cheer up the sad and make someone feel glad." When "doing good is a pleasure" (*Hymns*, 223), we are on the path of happiness, for "God loveth a cheerful giver" (2 Cor. 9:7).
- *Helping others receive the gift of eternal life* is the greatest gift we can give.
- "As you *submit your wills to God*, you are giving Him the *only* thing you can actually give Him that is really yours to give" (Maxwell, 46; italics added).
- "The greatest gift you could give to the Lord ... is to *keep yourself ... worthy to attend His holy house*. His gift to you will be the peace and security of knowing that you are worthy to meet Him, whenever that time shall come" (Nelson, 4; italics added).
- "Life is God's gift to man. What we do with our life is our gift to God" (Monson, 10; quoting Harold B. Lee).

We give these gifts when we keep our Sacrament covenant to "always remember [Christ] and keep his commandments which he has given [us]" (D&C 20:76). Seeing Christ in Christmas traditions helps us remember him when it is easy to forget. The two great *commandments* are to love God and our neighbor. The Christmas Spirit invites us to live these commandments.

Christ also gives us *personal commandments* "through the Holy Ghost" (Acts 1:2). After baptism, we are told to "receive the Holy Ghost," or in other words to follow our promptings and our conscience. One way to remember Christ is to ask, what would Jesus do (WWJD)? Jesus would seek to know and do the will of God through prayer, pondering which is "a form of prayer," scripture reading, and inspiration (Romney 1972, 4–5; 1973, 90).

Receiving Gifts: To receive "the greatest of all the gifts of God," one must come unto Christ, enter the strait gate of baptism, receive the Holy Ghost as a guide on the narrow path, continue on the path to the tree of life, partake of the fruit, be embraced like the returning prodigal, and enter into the rest or presence of the Lord (2 Ne. 33:9; D&C 84:23–24).

Journey's End © Derek J. Hegsted

To be embraced and taken back into the presence of God is not just to reconcile differences or to be forgiven, excused, or redeemed (debts or sins paid by another). It is being *one* with God and dwelling with him as a beloved daughter or son. A royal embrace occurred at the veil during an ancient Egyptian temple endowment (Nibley 1993, 249–257; 2005, 427–439). The embrace is a good symbol of *onement* (SOED physical union) and *atonement* or being *at one* (SOED unity of feeling, of one mind) or of one heart and mind with others.

"What doth it profit a man if a gift is bestowed upon him, and he receive not the gift? Behold, he rejoices not in that which is given unto him, neither rejoices in him who is the giver of the gift" (D&C 88:33). Christmas is a test to see if we will rejoice in our gifts and in the giver of each gift. As we open our gifts, we can be grateful or ungrateful for what we receive. If we are ungrateful, find fault with what we receive, or focus on what we did not receive, we will be unhappy. If we are grateful and express gratitude to the giver of each gift, we and they will be much happier. Alma said, "when thou risest in the morning let thy heart be full of thanks unto God" (Alma 37:37). When we obey the commandment to "thank the Lord thy God in all things" (D&C 59:7), we will learn that "some of God's greatest gifts are unanswered prayers" (Brooks). When we are satisfied with what we have, we are rich (Talmud, Mishnah, Pirke Avot 4:1, Ben Zoma). The apostle Paul was rich for he had "learned the secret of being content in any and every situation, whether well fed or hungry, whether living in plenty or in want" (NIV Philip. 4:11–13).

Real Meaning of Christmas: The reason for the season is to remember Christ and to become more like him.

- Christmas "is a season for giving and a time for gratitude. ... Christmas is more than trees and twinkling lights, more than toys and gifts. ... It is the love of the Son of God for all mankind. ... It is the peace which comforts, which sustains, which blesses all who accept it. ... In our times of grateful meditation, we acknowledge His priceless gift to us and pledge our love and faith. This is what Christmas is really about" (Hinckley 1997, 2).
- Christmas is *reminiscent* of the coming of the Savior in the meridian of time, to die for the sins of the world; and *prophetic* of the second coming when the risen and glorified Redeemer will reign upon the earth as King of kings (Hunter, 2).
- "What must we do this Christmas season—and always? ... We must do ... as the Wise Men of old. They sought out the Christ and found Him. ... Those who are wise still seek Him today" (Benson, 4).
- "During ... this Christmas season, find time to turn your heart to God. Perhaps ... in a quiet place, and on your knees—alone or with loved ones—give thanks for the good things that have come to you, and ask that his spirit might dwell in you as you earnestly strive to serve him and keep his commandments" (Hunter, 3).

Conclusion

As we look at a 3-D image, where we *focus* determines what we *see*, and what we *see* determines how we *feel*. "The mind can make a hell of heaven ... or a heaven of hell." The meanings we choose to *link* with Christmas traditions can help us remember or forget Christ at Christmas. Agency is the ability to choose what we see and do. As we learn to see Christ in *Christ*mas traditions, we can always remember Christ who is the reason for the season.

Gentle Christ © Del Parson

2

NATIVITY STORIES

Nativity stories, scenes, plays, art, and songs help us remember the birth of Jesus. During the Christmas season, families and churches put up nativity scenes, read the nativity story, and present nativity programs. Often children dress up and play the parts of Mary, Joseph, angels, shepherds, or wise men while the nativity story is read or Christmas songs are sung.

The nativity story can be more meaningful as we become aware of other versions of the story based on relevant historical and linguistic information. Writers and artists are like the six blind men who each felt different parts of an elephant. They recorded their observations of the size, shape, and flexibility of the part they felt.

Elephant and the Blind Men © Jain World

Then they shared their elephant "stories" that explained their observations. In the six stories, an elephant was like a wall, rope, tree, fan, spear, or snake. They all argued about which story was right (Saxe).

Elephant illustration © Jason Hunt

This story is comparable to our knowledge of the birth of Jesus. The New Testament only says that in Bethlehem, Mary "brought forth her firstborn son … and laid him in a manger; because there was no room for them in the inn" (Luke 2:7). To this account, writers and artists add *other information* (e.g., Bible language, customs, and history) and *imagination* to tell us different stories that answer questions about when and where Jesus was born.

On What Day Was Jesus Born?

December 25th is first found in records dated between AD 200 and 300. Scholars believe December 25th was picked to coincide with a popular pagan sun god festival that celebrated the victory of light over darkness just after the shortest day of the year (Hunter, 2; Walker, 154–55; *Encyclopedia of Mormonism*, s.v. "April 6"). Others have noted that St. Augustine (c. AD 354–430) wrote that Jesus was conceived on March 25th (the day He died) and was born exactly 9 months later on December 25th (Pratt 1990, 8–14; Walker, 154–55).

Passover is when Jewish tradition expected the Messiah to come. Passover is "a night to be much observed unto the Lord" (a night of watching) because *"on that night Messiah* and Elijah will be made great" or *will appear* (Lehrman, 227–28; italics added). According to Jewish tradition, Isaac, a son of Abraham, "was born on the first day of Passover. At his birth ... the sun shone with unparalleled splendor, the like of which will only be seen again in the messianic age" (*Encyclopedia Judaica*, s.v. "Isaac").

Each Jewish month began when the moon was first visible after the new moon. Thus, the 15th of each month was a full moon. Passover night is the 15th of Nisan during a full moon between March 21st and April 23rd.

During the weeks before Passover, shepherds watched their flocks by night because it was lambing season. Passover was symbolic of Christ's *coming* and crucifixion (Pratt 1994, 38–45). During Passover, the population of Jerusalem went from about 30,000 to about 300,000 or more. People camped out on hillsides or stayed with people in Jerusalem or in surrounding areas (Sanders, 126–9). Christ was crucified during Passover almost exactly 33 "Nephite years" after he was born (3 Ne. 8:5). Thus, he was also born during this season (Ogden and Skinner, 773). This is like the Jewish tradition that Abraham, Isaac, and Jacob died in the same month they were born (Talmud, Rosh Hashanah, http://www.jewishvirtuallibrary.org/jsource/Talmud/rh1.html; search for "were born").

April 6th is the day Jesus was born according to LDS prophets. On April 6, 1830, the Church was organized, 1,830 "years since the coming of our Lord and Savior Jesus Christ in the flesh" (D&C 20:1). President Lee said, "April 6, 1973, … commemorates not only the anniversary of the organization of The Church …, but also the anniversary of the birth of … Jesus Christ" (Lee, 2). President Kimball said, "Today [April 6, 1980] we not only celebrate … the organization of the Church, but also … the birth of Christ on this day 1,980 years ago" (Kimball, 54).

In What Year Was Jesus Born?

Some LDS scholars believe Jesus was born exactly 1,830 years before April 6, 1830. Others believe Jesus was born four years earlier and that the phrase 1,830 "years since the coming of our Lord" simply expressed the current year as being 1830. Elder Bruce R. McConkie wrote in 1979, "We do not believe it is possible with the present state of our knowledge … to state with finality" the year Jesus was born (McConkie, I:349–350). He then summarized the two positions. A review of the evidence and arguments for these positions is found in *When Was Jesus Born, Baptized, and Buried?* (Shelley).

5 or 4 BC is the year Jesus was born according to most scholars today. The four gospels agree that Jesus was born before King Herod died. Most scholars believe King Herod died in 4 BC. Elder McConkie and President J. Reuben Clark used 5 or 4 BC in their writings to help LDS students who would be referring to Bible commentaries by scholars who used that date. However, they did not believe it was "a settled issue" (McConkie, I:349–350).

1 BC is 1,830 years before the Church was organized. After examining astronomical and historical evidence, some scholars believe King Herod could have died between 4 BC and AD 1 (Pratt 1990, 8–14). April 6, 1 BC was Passover night. Jesus "began to be about thirty years of age" shortly after John the Baptist began his ministry in AD 29 (Luke 3:1, 23). Levites who were "thirty years old and upward" entered into the service of the Lord (Num. 4:3, 23, 30). April 6, AD 30 was during Passover week when Jesus turned 30, cleansed the temple, and began his public ministry. Scholars agree that AD 33 is one of the years that fit the evidence for the crucifixion (Shelley). According to the Book of Mormon, Jesus lived 33 years and died at the start of his 34th year (3 Ne. 8:5; Ogden and Skinner, 773).

Where Was Jesus Born?

Prophecies: Nephi said, 600 "years from the time that my father left Jerusalem, a prophet would the Lord God raise up *among the Jews* — even a Messiah, or ... a Savior of the world" (1 Ne. 10:3). "Lehi may also have left Jerusalem at Passover because the time was linked to the birth of Christ (1 Ne. 19:8) and he was also delivered from bondage (Alma 36:28–29), led through the wilderness (Alma 9:9; D&C 17:1), and crossed the water to a promised land (1 Ne. 5:5)" (Pratt 1994, 45, note 7).

Micah said, "Bethlehem ... out of thee shall he come forth unto me that is to be ruler in Israel" (Micah 5:2). Alma said, "He shall be born of Mary, *at Jerusalem* which is the *land* of our forefathers, she being a virgin ... who shall ... bring forth a son, yea, even the Son of God" (Alma 7:10). The "*land* of Jerusalem" included both the city of Jerusalem and the city of Bethlehem (Bennett).

Journey to Bethlehem: Jesus was born in Bethlehem, which is five miles south of Jerusalem and 92 miles south of Nazareth. Joseph and Mary probably travelled down the Jordan Valley to Jericho instead of going through Samaria. "From Jericho through the desert to Bethlehem is an uphill hike of 3,300 feet." It would have taken Mary and Joseph four or five days to travel from Nazareth to Bethlehem (Ogden and Skinner, 51–53).

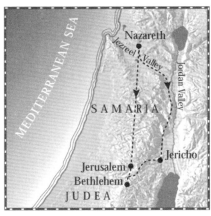

Two likely routes © D. Kelly Ogden

Journey to Bethlehem © Joseph Brickey

Why Bethlehem? Jesus, the "bread of life," was born in Bethlehem, which means "house of bread." The Messiah, the Son of David, was born in Bethlehem, the City of David, where David had been a shepherd and watched over his flocks (1 Sam. 17:15). The photograph below shows Bethlehem in the "hill country of Judæa" (Luke 1:65) as seen from the southern border of Jerusalem.

Bethlehem and Shepherds' Fields © D. Kelly Ogden

No Room in the Inn

In Luke we read, "While they were there, the days were accomplished that she should be delivered. And she brought forth her firstborn son, and wrapped him in swaddling clothes, and laid him in a manger; because there was no room for them in the inn" (Luke 2:6–7) or "inns" (JST).

Writers and artists use *other information* and their *imagination* to tell the rest of the story. For example, modern cities have more than one hotel or motel where travelers can rent rooms from an "innkeeper." "No Vacancy" signs indicate when a motel is full. Perhaps such information along with the writer's imagination led to the following story. Notice that the italicized phrases are not in the Bible account.

💬 **Stable Story:** "So many people had come to Bethlehem to pay their taxes that Mary and Joseph *couldn't find a place to stay*. Finally, *an innkeeper* told them that *his inn was full*, but they could *stay in his stables*. Mary and Joseph *thanked the innkeeper* for his kindness. *That night Jesus was born*" (Buck; italics added).

No Room at the Inn © Northumberland

About AD 1223, St. Francis of Assisi did a live nativity scene in a stable with animals, people, hay, and a manger like those of his time. Since then, most nativity scenes show Joseph and Mary in a stable or wooden building with stalls in which domestic animals are sheltered and fed. In these scenes, baby Jesus is in a wooden manger.

For God So Loved the World © Simon Dewey

This popular and familiar story is often portrayed in Christmas art, plays and programs to help people remember the birth of Christ. In Mexico, families reenact Joseph and Mary looking for lodging (*posada*). On each of the nine nights before Christmas, families carry figurines of Joseph and Mary and request lodging at three homes or "inns." The first two "innkeepers" turn them away. After the last "innkeeper" lets them in, the guests pray before a nativity scene, sing Christmas songs, and have a party that includes a *piñata* for the children.

Caravansary or Khan

Khan or Caravansary, photo by Babak Gholizadeh

The Good Samaritan took a wounded man to a *pandocheíon*, a public inn called a *caravansary* or *khan* (Luke 10:34). Some scholars believe the "inn" in the nativity story was a caravansary "built to accommodate travelers who traversed the route between Jerusalem and Egypt" (Black, 19). A caravansary was somewhat like a fort for caravans with only one big gate for an entrance. Rooms without furniture were along the four sides. Animals were kept in the center courtyard. Travelers cared for their own animals and brought their own food and supplies. Innkeepers charged little for shelter but were paid extra for other services, as in the story of the Good Samaritan (*International Standard Bible Encyclopedia*, s.v. "Inn"). "Prostitution was part of the system. This explains why Jesus told his disciples to seek accommodation in private homes (Matt. 10:11)" and why Christian hospitality was important (Rom. 12:13, Gower, 234).

💬 **Hillside Cave Story:** "If travelers reached the inn [caravansary] early in the day, they were usually welcomed by the innkeeper. If they arrived in the evening, the door was closed for protection and travelers were encouraged to move along. *Arriving in the evening* and unwelcome by the *innkeeper*, Joseph searched for lodging in the ... hillsides that bordered Bethlehem." *In a hillside cave* that sheltered animals, Mary "brought forth her firstborn son" (Black, 19; italics added).

Silent Night (in a cave) © Liz Lemon Swindle

💬 **Caravansary Courtyard Story:** If a traveler arrived late at the caravansary "and the *leewans* [rooms] were all occupied by earlier guests, he would have no choice but to be content with such accommodation as he could find in the courtyard below, and secure for himself and his family such small amount of cleanliness and decency as are compatible with an unoccupied corner on the filthy area, which he would be obliged to share with horses, mules, and camels" (Farrar 1874, 37; quoted in McConkie, I:343–344 and referred to in IV:22).

💬 **Private Home Story:** Mary and Joseph stayed in the stable portion of a home below the family's dwelling area. The idea that they stayed in the stables of the inn "is unthinkable to any who know the East and the ... hospitality of its people" (Whiting[3] 1929, 730; see picture on 719; 1914, 251, 253).

Kataluma

The Greek word for "inn" was *kataluma* (Luke 2:7), not *pandocheíon* (*caravansary*), which Luke used in the Good Samaritan story (Luke 10:34). *Kataluma* is used in only two other places in the Bible (see Mark 14:14; Luke 22:11). There it is translated as "guestchamber" and refers to the "upper room" in a private house used for the Last Supper (*International Standard Bible Encyclopedia*, s.v. "Inn").

💬 **Caravansary Guestrooms Story:** Elder McConkie (I:343–344) quoted Farrar's 1874 courtyard story. Since the JST has *inns* instead of *inn*, he then suggested that Jesus was born in the courtyard because "there was no room in any of the inns or guestchambers that surrounded and opened upon the open courtyard" (McConkie, IV:22). Elder McConkie also said, "unless or until some of the saints ... see in a dream or a vision the inn where Joseph and Mary and Jesus spent that awesome night, we can only speculate as to the details" (I:344).

---

[3] John D. Whiting was "born in Jerusalem. ... [He] was an expert on the topography, history, and local customs of the Holy Land. ... *The National Geographic* published several of his articles on Palestine" (http://www.loc.gov/exhibits/americancolony/amcolony-locust.html).

Some scholars argue that *kataluma* can refer to a public inn while others say it refers to a private guest room. However, there is no linguistic evidence or argument that *kataluma* referred to individual rooms in a *caravansary* or *khan*.[4]

Hospitality: "Because Jewish people had received protection from God, they were to give protection to others. ... The Jews believed that God sometimes sent angels in disguise to test whether people were obeying the law of hospitality. ... A stranger would normally go to the gate or wait by the well until an invitation to stay had been given by someone locally. ... In a larger house ... a guest room would be provided" (Gower, 241, 243–4).

Extended Family: "The family in traditional societies is made up of an extended group of people, with a patriarch [or *sheikh*] at the head. Married children and their children usually lived with or near the father and mother. The authority and protection of the father extended to them, and their respect and obedience were expected in return (cf. Luke 15). Relatives from other towns were welcomed by the patriarch and brought under his protection during their stay in his village" (Pfann).

---

[4] Farrar (1874) and Edersheim (1883, 185) are frequently quoted by Elder McConkie. They both believed the inn (*kataluma*) referred to a public inn (caravansary or khan). Elder McConkie also quotes often from Geikie (1891) who says that *kataluma* refers to a private guest room instead of a public inn (Geikie 85). Edersheim argues that *kataluma* can also refer to a public inn based on how it was used in the LXX or Greek Septuagint (Greek translation of the Hebrew Old Testament). However, the LXX does not use the more specific word *pandocheíon* (public inn or caravansary) used by Luke.

House built over a cave used as a stable,[5] photo by American Colony Photographers, Jerusalem

Family Homes: "The architecture of the family home ... made provision for the occasional guest. The most common dwelling was the courtyard home which was multi-leveled. A lower room or cellar was used as a storeroom. In the hilly areas like Bethlehem, a cave adjacent to the courtyard might often be adapted for this purpose. Here the family's prized or more vulnerable animals could be fed and sheltered at night, protected from the cold, thieves and predators. The main living area, partitioned into several sections, was on an upper level. It had a work and kitchen area, where children often slept, and a separate bedroom for the parents. In a wealthier home, a third room would be added for guests and for entertaining." *Kataluma* "may have referred to this room in the family home" (Pfann).

---

[5] "Many of these dwellings, placed as they are on ancient sites, are built over old caves or caverns, which are incorporated with the lower or stable portion" (Whiting 1914, 310).

💬 ***Kataluma* Story:** Joseph and Mary went to Bethlehem, the land of Joseph's ancestors. "When they arrived, Joseph most likely went straight to his paternal home, seeking the help and protection of his relatives currently living there, and received it, for Mary was pregnant and Jewish custom would demand such a response." "*While they were there*, the days were accomplished that she should be delivered" (Luke 2:6). However, the guest room (*kataluma*) was "full of relatives and no private place existed for her to deliver her baby. No private place, that is, until someone had the bright and compassionate idea to suggest that she could have the baby down below, away from the crowded kataluma, in the warmth of the storeroom and animal's cellar, and yet still be within the security of the family home" (Pfann; Holzapfel, Huntsman, and Wayment, 109; Brown, 115; Geikie, 85; *International Standard Bible Encyclopedia*, s.v. "Inn").

The Church of the Nativity is the traditional site of the birth of Jesus. It is in the middle of Bethlehem "where the family homes would have stood in antiquity, and not in the surrounding countryside" (Pfann).

Church of the Nativity © D. Kelly Ogden

A second century source says Jesus was born in a cave (Holzapfel, Huntsman, and Wayment, 109; Brown, 15–6). "The Grotto of the Nativity, an underground cave located beneath the [Church of the Nativity], enshrines the site where Jesus is said to have been born. The exact spot is marked beneath an altar by a 14-pointed silver star set into the marble floor and surrounded by silver lamps. This altar is denominationally neutral, although it features primarily Armenian Apostolic influences. Another altar [on the right] …, which is maintained by the Roman Catholics, marks the site where traditionally Mary laid the newborn Baby in the manger" (http://en.wikipedia.org/wiki/Church_of_the_Nativity).

Grotto of the Nativity © D. Kelly Ogden

Lydia Mountford was born in Jerusalem in 1848 and learned the *oral traditions* of peasant shepherds in Christian villages who kept their ancient customs, costumes, and traditions (Whiting 1926, 729; 1914, 249, 270). Many of the oral traditions she shares are found in ancient writings while others are not. She was invited to give lectures in the tabernacle and throughout Utah in 1897. (See the Appendix for more information about this interesting lady.) Mountford says, "our legends say that Jesus was born in a grotto [cave]. ... If Jesus was born in that grotto which they show you today, we know that that is the spot, because there is no other inn in the place. ... Bethlehem is a small place, and that inn has been there from time immemorial. ... It was the home originally of Boaz, who was a wealthy man. And then Obed was born there, and Jesse, and David was born in that very house. ... Jesus was born in that very property, in that very spot where, according to legend, David had been crowned king of the shepherds in the olden time" (Mountford 1911, 26–28).

If Jesus was born in this cave, was it part of a private home (Pfann) or part of an inn as Mountford suggests? We do not know.

Birth of Jesus

Mary "brought forth her firstborn son, and wrapped him in swaddling clothes, and laid him in a manger" (Luke 2:7).

Midwives: During Bible times, midwives typically delivered babies. They are specifically mentioned in the time of Isaac, Jacob, and Moses (Gen. 35:17; 38:28; Ex. 1). It is likely that a midwife helped with the delivery of the Christ child (Brown, 115 n. 59).

Rubbed with Salt: After cutting the umbilical cord, "the new-born child is then bathed ... [and] the body was rubbed with salt ... not merely for the purpose of making the skin drier and firmer, or of cleansing it more thoroughly, but probably from a regard to the virtue of salt as a protection from putrification" (Keil and Delitzsch, 9:197).

Swaddling Clothes: Some artwork depicts the baby Jesus wrapped up like a mummy.

The Birth of Jesus by Barna Da Siena

"For years the Orientals of Bible lands have cared for an infant child much as it was done when Jesus was born. Instead of allowing the young baby the free use of its limbs, it is bound hand and foot by swaddling bands, and thus made into a helpless bundle like a mummy. At birth the child is washed and rubbed with salt, and then with its legs together, and its arms at its side, it is wound around tightly with linen or cotton bandages, four to five inches wide, and five to six yards long. The band is placed under the chin and over the forehead" (Wight, 108–109). "Babies are kept salted for a week, and swaddled for from four to six months. ... This salting and swaddling are supposed to benefit and strengthen the child for life, and none is thought properly cared for if the procedure is omitted" (Whiting 1929, 727, 730).

Mother holding baby in swaddling clothes, photo by American Colony

In 1929, the picture above was published. It shows a mother of the village of Judea holding her child wrapped in swaddling clothes that are not mummylike (Whiting, 1929, 711). "Oriental swaddling-clothes consist of a *square of cloth* and two or more *bandages*. The child is laid on the cloth diagonally and the corners are folded over the feet and body and under the head, the bandages then being tied so as to hold the cloth in position. This device forms the clothing of the child until it is about a year old, and its omission (Ezek. 16:4) would be a token that the child had been abandoned" (*International Standard Bible Encyclopedia*, 1960, s.v. "Swaddle"; italics added).

Swaddling Bands in "Savior of the World" © Intellectual Reserve, Inc.

The swaddling bandages or bands were "embroidered with symbols indicating family history and genealogy. According to ancient and modern custom, the embroidery, to be acceptable, must be exactly the same on both sides. This was a type showing that the outward life and the inner life were the same—they were never to have a 'wrong side' to their character" (Nielsen, 35–36). "Mary was from the tribe of Judah, so she may have used symbols common to that lineage such as a lion, a lamb, or a tree of life. As a descendant of David, she was also entitled to use the royal colors of blue and white" (http://www.lds.org/pa/display/0,17884,7244-1,00.html). "Under the wedding canopy, these decorated bands would be tied around the clasped right hands on the bride and groom; hence the saying, 'They tied the knot.' These bands would later be used to fasten the swaddling clothes of their children" (Nielsen, 35–36).

Manger: About AD 1223, St. Francis of Assisi did a live nativity scene with animals, people, hay, and a manger like those of his time. Since then, most nativity scenes show Joseph and Mary in a stable of wood with the baby Jesus in a wooden manger or feeding trough. However, the manger was likely made of stone or carved out of a cave wall and measured "three to four feet in length. The cavity that usually held fodder for animals would be just the right size and ... height for a baby! (The phrase, "born in a manger," is unscriptural.)" (Hulbert; *Harper's Bible Dictionary* 1985, s.v. "Manger"; *The Interpreter's Dictionary of the Bible* 1962, s.v. "Manger"). Jesus was not born in a manger. Mary *"laid* him in a manger" (Luke 2:7).

Below is a picture of a stone manger taken in the ruins of Megiddo, an ancient city mentioned in the Bible. Some nativity scenes have a stone manger in a cave.[6]

Stone manger at Meggido, photo by Darko Tepert Donatus

---

[6] See photograph of the 2007 nativity scene on Temple Square in Salt Lake City, Utah (http://www.tommysimms.com). See also Biblequest's "Birth of Jesus: Joseph, Mary & Jesus."

Evergreens: "There must have been beautiful flowers and evergreens and palm trees. For every child that is born in the East, a wreath of evergreen and a potted palm is brought ... to show that it is an immortal soul. ... There will be also ... a seven-branched candlestick," or menorah (Mountford 1911, 38).

Shepherds Watching Their Flock

Bible: "There were in the same country shepherds abiding in the field, keeping watch over their flock by night. And ... the angel ... said ..., Fear not ... For unto you is born this day in the city of David a Savior, which is Christ the Lord. [Aramaic: who is YHWH, the Messiah] And this shall be a sign ...; Ye shall find the babe wrapped in swaddling clothes, lying in a manger. ... And ... the shepherds ... came with haste, and found Mary, and Joseph, and the babe lying in a manger"(Luke 2:8–16).

The Announcement of Christ's Birth to the Shepherds by Del Parson
© Intellectual Reserve, Inc.

Modern Times: Before Passover, shepherds are out at night watching their flocks on the hillsides because it is lambing season. Shepherds bring their flocks to the sheepfolds, comprised of natural caves around which walls of loose stones have been built. Here, they watch to make sure the ewes do not lose any of their lambs while giving birth (Barney).

Who Were the Shepherds? These were not ordinary shepherds or flocks. According to Jewish tradition, the Messiah would be revealed from *Migdal Eder* (tower of the flock), a tower near Bethlehem. From this tower, shepherds guarded their sheep that were to be sacrificed at the temple (Edersheim, 186–187; McConkie, I:347; Black, 19–20). The "Lamb of God" was born among the animals during the lambing season as were other lambs that would become Passover sacrifices. Also the birth of the "Good Shepherd" was first announced to shepherds.

The Good Shepherd © Del Parson

The Sign: "Ye shall find the babe wrapped in swaddling clothes, lying in a manger ... The shepherds ... came with haste, and found Mary, and Joseph, and the babe lying in a manger" (Luke 2:12). In English, *manger* is "a box or trough in a stable ... from which ... cattle eat" (SOED). The Greek word, *phátnē*, translated as *manger*, can mean *manger* or *stall* (*BAG*). Were the shepherds given more directions? If not, how many stables or caves did they search before they found the babe lying in a manger? Since most babies would be wrapped in swaddling clothes, how would they know it was the right baby?

Birth of Jesus © Del Parson

💬 **Caravansary and Shepherd Story:** According to legend, "there were twelve babies in the mangers when Jesus was born in Bethlehem. ... And how would you know one baby from another, except by the ensign and the swaddling clothes of its clan and its tribe? ... So the shepherds came to them, and bowed low before Joseph and Mary ... and brought their offerings of lambs and laid them before the child. ... And the chief shepherd says, "a great angel ... said to us, '... you shall find Him wrapped in swaddling clothes, in the plaid of the King of the Shepherds' " (Mountford 1911, 39–41).

💬 **Migdal Eder Story:** "There was no need for the angel to give these shepherds directions. ... [They raised] lambs that were sacrificed in the Temple. ... The sign of a manger could only mean their manger at the tower of the flock ... where there were ceremonially clean stalls, carefully maintained by Temple priests who oversaw the birth of each lamb. 'Migdal Eder' (tower of the flock) at Bethlehem is the perfect place for Christ to be born. ... Jesus was not born behind an inn, in a smelly stable" with donkeys and other animals. "He was born in Bethlehem, at the birthing place of the sacrificial lambs that were offered in the Temple in Jerusalem which Micah 4:8 calls the 'tower of the flock,' " or Migdal Eder (Abrams).

Israel Buries Rachel: The meanings of the Hebrew names in the Old Testament account of Rachel's burial suggest interesting parallels with the nativity story. "And they journeyed from **Beth-el** [*House of God*]; ... and **Rachel** [*ewe or female sheep*] ... had hard labor. ... As her soul was in departing, (for she died) she called his name **Ben-oni** [*son of my sorrow*]: but his father called him **Benjamin** [*son at the right hand*]. Rachel ... was buried in the way to **Ephrath** [*fruitfulness*], which *is* **Beth-lehem** [*house of bread*]. ... And **Israel** [*God prevails* or *man seeing God*[7]] ... spread

---

[7] Some believe that Israel (yiśrā'ēl) comes from "śārāh 'ēl" which means "God persists or prevails" (*BDB*, s.v. "יִשְׂרָאֵל"; *BD*, s.v. "Israel"). However, Origen says that Israel means "man seeing God" (Origen, *De Principiis*, 4.2.22 [*ANF* 4]; Origen, *Commentary on John*, 2.25 [*ANF* 9]) which would come from "yiś rā'āh 'ēl." Both meanings fit the context which says, "thy name shall be called no more Jacob, but Israel: for... thou... hast *prevailed*. ... And Jacob... [said] I have *seen God face to face*" (Gen. 32:28, 30).

his tent beyond **Migdal Eder** [*tower of the flock*]" (Gen. 35:16–21). Like Benjamin, Jesus was Mary's "son of sorrow" during the crucifixion and was later seen standing on "the right hand" of God.

Name and Blessing

Jesus was circumcised eight days after birth. Usually the firstborn was named after the paternal grandfather. However, the babe was named Jesus (*Yeshua*) which means Savior or salvation. Jesus entered the covenant of Abraham once he received his name (Black, 23).

Temple Offering

"And when the days of her purification according to the law of Moses were accomplished, they brought him to Jerusalem, to present him to the Lord; (As it is written in the law …, Every male that openeth the womb shall be called holy to the Lord;) And to offer a sacrifice according to that which is said in the law of the Lord, A pair of turtledoves, or two young pigeons" (Luke 2:22–24).

> The old Levitical law was that they were to bring a lamb to be sacrificed for the redemption of the soul of the child, and *doves and pigeons were brought as an offering and atonement for the mother*. The Levitical law went on to say that if the parents were too poor to bring a lamb, they could omit the lamb, and they must bring the doves and the pigeons; and we have jumped to the conclusion that they could not afford to bring the lamb. …
>
> Mary could not possibly have been so poor as not to bring a lamb, because a lamb in that country costs only fifty cents. But suppose she was too poor to pay the fifty cents, how about the shepherds that came? Every shepherd that comes to pay you an ordinary visit must bring you a lamb as a present in his bosom. But at the birth they must bring three: one to be sacrificed for the body, one for the soul, and one for the spirit. Now, every

shepherd that came up to the birth of Jesus must have brought three lambs. ...

How about Zacharias? He was a chief priest of the city of Jerusalem. He was a wealthy man. ... He had hundreds of lambs grazing on the hillsides. Would he allow his niece Mary to come to Jerusalem with the Christ as a pauper, without having a lamb? ...

So it was not because she was poor that Mary does not bring the lamb. ... The lamb was typical of Jesus Christ. Jesus Christ Himself, the Lamb of God, had come to be sacrificed, and how could He be redeemed by the sacrifice of a lamb? ...

Now, here comes Mary, bringing this child into the temple. ... The legends tell us that as she stood at the entrance of the temple, she wept as she looked upon this beautiful baby ...; she kissed it ... and said: "... I would gladly give a thousand lambs, let them all be slain, for Him ... Strengthen my heart, O Lord! ... Must I give Him up as the Lamb of God, not as the lambs ... but as a living sacrifice?" ...

Mary enters [the temple. And Simeon] ... dedicated Him as the Lamb of God. (Mountford 1911, 47–53, 56–57; italics added)

Wise Men

Bible: "When Jesus was born in Bethlehem ..., there came wise men *from the east* to Jerusalem, Saying, Where is he that is born King of the Jews? for we have seen his star in the east, and are come to worship him. When Herod ... had gathered all the chief priests and scribes ..., he demanded of them where Christ should be born. They said ..., In Bethlehem ... [as] written by [Micah]. ... The star, which [the wise men] saw in the east, went before them. ... And when they were come into the *house*, they saw the *young child* with Mary his mother, and fell down, and worshipped him: and ... they presented unto him gifts; gold, and frankincense, and myrrh" (Matt. 2:1–11).

"Herod, when he saw that he was mocked of the wise men, was exceeding wroth, ... and slew all the children that were in Bethlehem, ... from *two years old and under*, according to the time which he had diligently enquired of the wise men" (Matt. 2:16).

Wise Men Follow the Star by Paul Mann © Intellectual Reserve, Inc.

What was the star? In the Bible account, there is no indication that anyone but the wise men saw the star or understood its meaning. Was the star mythical, miraculous or an actual light in the heavens (e.g., star, planets, comet)? Scholars give different answers. Those who believe it was an actual light also consider planets (wandering stars) to be possibilities. Scholars suggest different events depending on when they believe Jesus was born (Shelley). These celestial sights would have been recognized by those who studied the stars. "An early Christian document indicates that [the star] was an angel in the guise of a star (see *1 Infancy Gospel* 3:3)" (Tvedtnes).

Wise Men Bearing Gifts by Paul Mann © Intellectual Reserve, Inc.

When did the wise men come? Many people and artists assume that the wise men arrived soon after Jesus was born. However, scholars note that he could have been a "young child" nearing two years old because Herod had children "two years old and under" killed based on what the wise men told him. Since the wise men came after Jesus was born and before Herod died, most scholars place the visit of the wise men within three to nine months after Jesus was born (Shelley).

The Holy Men © Liz Lemon Swindle

How many wise men were there? According to oral tradition, "there were seven wise men, but three ... were representative of professions" (Mountford 1911, 71). "Some early traditions indicate there were twelve Wise Men. The most prevalent tradition says they were three kings, their number derived from the three gifts they brought: gold, frankincense, and myrrh" (Tvedtnes; *BD*, s.v. "Magi").

Who were the wise men? "Their spiritual capacity is evident: They were able to see the star when others could not; they knew its meaning. ... It seems likely that they were representatives of a branch of the Lord's people somewhere from east of Palestine, who had come, led by the Spirit, to behold the Son of God, and who returned to their people to bear witness that the King Immanuel had ... been born in the flesh" (*BD*, s.v. "Magi").

Some believe the wise men came from Babylon, which was part of Persia (Tvedtnes). About 600 years earlier, Nebuchadnezzar put Daniel in charge of "all the wise men of Babylon" (Dan. 2:48). *Magi*, the Greek word for 'wise men,' referred to wise men and priests who were expert in astrology or astronomy and interpretation of dreams (*BAG*, s.v. Μάγος). A few years later, Nebuchadnezzar "carried away all Jerusalem, and all the princes, and all the *mighty men of valor*, even *ten thousand* captives, and all the *craftsmen and smiths*: *none remained, save the poorest sort of the people* of the land. And he carried away [king] Jehoiachin to Babylon, ... and his officers, and the *mighty of the land* ... And all the *men of might* ... [and] all that were *strong and apt for war*" (2 Kgs. 24:14–16). About 480 BC, Esther married king Ahasuerus, a Persian, and saved her Jewish people (Esther 2–5). According to tradition, Mary's father was a descendant of Esther and her Persian husband. Mary's mother was a descendant of the royal line, through Solomon, and a descendant of Ephraim who was a son of Joseph, a ruler of Egypt, and Princess Asenath of Egypt (Mountford 1911, 14–17). After Cyrus conquered Babylon about 539 BC, he let Jews return to Jerusalem to rebuild the temple. However, most Jews stayed in Babylon or Persia. "According to our unwritten history, these wise men were priests from Persia; they were Magian princes from the great Magian order, and they came to worship Christ, to take their oath of allegiance to Him" (Mountford 1911, 68).

Gifts of the wise men: One writer suggests that the gifts indicated the professions of the wise men.

> *Gold* ... represents to us kings, *frankincense* means priests, and *myrrh* means scientific men. So these wise men were representatives of kings, priests, and scientists, and for once in their lives these three great powers united together ... to do honor to Christ. These wise men were great astronomers and astrologers. ... They ... opened their vessels of gold, frankincense, and myrrh ... each one wearing the garment of his profession or rank. There were seven wise men, but three of them were representatives of professions. ... First ... came the representative of the *king*; and ... he brought a crown. ... Then came the great *priests*, the wise men, ... the Magians; and ... brought their offering of incense. ... Then came the great *scientific men* ... and they laid the myrrh before Him to signify that they had looked to find the source of life in everything that was created. ... And so these three men bowed before Him ... and took their oath of allegiance and worshipped Him. (Mountford 1911, 68, 71–72; italics added)

We Three Kings © Simon Dewey

Other writers suggest that "the gifts presented to Jesus were symbols of his royal destiny" (Black, 27–28).

- *Gold* became the customary gift to acknowledge royalty. (Jesus was the *King of Kings*.)
- *Frankincense* was used in ritual sacrifice at the Temple Mount. (Jesus was the *Great High Priest*.)
- *Myrrh* was a painkiller offered to Christ on the cross (Mark 15:23) and an embalming ingredient used in His burial (John 19:39). (Jesus was the *Redeemer*.)
- *Myrrh* was also an ingredient in the holy anointing oil used to consecrate people and things to make them sacred or holy (Ex. 39:22–29; Barker 2004, 57–58, 91–92). *Messiah* (Hebrew) and *Christ* (Greek) mean *Anointed*. (Jesus was the *Messiah*, the *Holy One of Israel*.)

Which of the Stories Is Correct?

We have reviewed the following stories of the birth of Jesus:
1. Stable story
2. Hillside cave story
3. Caravansary courtyard story
4. Private home story
5. Caravansary guestrooms story
6. Kataluma (guest room) story
7. Caravansary and shepherd story
8. Migdal Eder story

There are variations for each story. We do not know for sure which one or ones may be true. However, it is likely the manger referred to a stone feeding trough in a cave rather than a wooden trough in a stable.

Several of these stories assume the inn was a caravansary with an innkeeper. However, there is no archaeological evidence of a caravansary near Bethlehem. Also, the Greek word is *kataluma* (guest room) not *pandocheíon* (caravansary). The "caravansary guestrooms story" suggests that *kataluma* may have referred to rooms in a caravansary. However, there is no linguistic evidence of *kataluma* referring to these rooms.

If the patriarch or sheikh owned the sheep being watched from Migdal Eder, the *kataluma* and Migdal Eder stories could be combined.

Conclusion

The Bible account of the birth of Jesus leaves much room for writers and artists to add *other information* and *imagination* as they share their stories to help us remember Christ. Several of these stories provide interesting alternatives to the common nativity stories depicted in Christmas programs, plays, and art.

Perhaps, the question is not which story or stories are correct, but which stories help us understand, remember, and appreciate the birth of Jesus? All of these stories help me reflect on the birth of Jesus, the king of kings, in very humble surroundings. Some stories use familiar images of inns, innkeepers, wooden stables and mangers which help me appreciate the humble circumstances of the birth of Jesus. Other stories help me understand more about the culture and language of the people in Israel at the time of the birth of Jesus. I enjoy paintings that reflect the different stories because they help me remember Christ and imagine the events depicted.

Elder Bruce R. McConkie said, "unless or until some of the saints ... see in a dream or a vision the inn where Joseph and Mary and Jesus spent that awesome night, we can only *speculate* as to the details" (McConkie, I:344; italics added). However, we do know that Jesus was born of Mary, was baptized by John, taught and healed the people, called twelve apostles, established his church, atoned for the sins of men, was crucified on the cross, was resurrected, appeared to his apostles in the old world, appeared to the Nephites in the new world, and appeared to Joseph Smith in the sacred grove. His birth, life, teachings, death, and resurrection changed the world. This is the reason we remember birth of Christ each Christmas season.

When God wants to change the world,
He sends a child.

She Shall Bring Forth A Son © Liz Lemon Swindle

3

ADVENT TREES AND CALENDARS

I attended a BYU Education Week class in 2007 by Donna B. Nielsen entitled "Explore the Family Tree of Christ: The Heritage of Jesus in Advent Stories and Symbols." She discussed the history of Jesse trees as well as advent trees and advent calendars. She then discussed how parents have adapted this idea to help their children remember Christ at Christmas. I was excited to see her examples and shared them with my wife who was familiar with traditional advent calendars. My wife was intrigued with the possibilities for helping our family focus on and remember Christ. Last Christmas we bought a small tree and shared the ideas with our children and grandchildren.

I did an internet search for "Jesse trees" and "advent trees" to learn more.[8] Jesse trees are based on Isaiah's prophecy, "A shoot will come up from the stump of Jesse; from his roots a Branch will bear fruit" (NIV Isa. 11:1). Jesse was the father of David and the "Branch" refers to Christ (Jer. 23:5). Pictures of a Jesse tree show a symbolic tree with branches representing the genealogy of Christ. A Jesse tree uses stories and images to remind us of the

---

[8] Some fun websites include: http://www.cresourcei.org/jesse.html; http://www.domestic-church.com/content.dcc/19971201/fridge/fridge1.htm; http://www.christiancrafters.com/jesse_tree.html.

ancestors of Christ (e.g., Jesse, David, Ruth) and God's dealings with them.

Advent means *arrival* or *coming* and refers to the season including the four Sundays immediately preceding Christmas. Traditional advent calendars have a picture with twenty-four "doors." Children open one "door" each day from December 1st to the 24th. Behind each "door" is a picture related to the nativity or Christmas symbols (e.g., bells, holly).

Advent Calendar

For advent trees, some families use a small tree while others use a flannel tree. Each day they put on the tree a handmade ornament or inexpensive object representing scriptural events ranging from the creation to the birth of Christ. Ornaments may be pictures or drawings on a piece of thick paper. They can be made and discussed in family home evenings. When children add ornaments to the tree, they explain what the symbol represents to them.

Donna gave examples of ornaments that illustrated several scriptural topics such as the following:
1. Events from the creation to the birth of Jesus.
2. Stories about the ancestors of Jesus (e.g., Jesse, David, Ruth) to make a Jesse Tree.
3. Titles of Christ.
4. Teachings of Christ.
5. Favorite scriptures.
6. Events related to the second coming, or *advent*, of Jesus.

Given this list of possible topics, it was easy to see how a family could make one or more sets of 24 different inexpensive ornaments. Each member of the family could make his or her own ornaments. They could each take turns selecting, explaining, and placing a daily family ornament on the tree, or each person could explain and put on a different daily ornament.

Advent Tree

Nature Ornaments

While serving as a scoutmaster for several years, I had the privilege of camping in the outdoors ten or more nights each year with scouts and other leaders. We hiked and camped in wilderness areas where we saw many types of plants and animals. We enjoyed hiking in the mountains, camping near streams or lakes, and sleeping in snow caves. Scouts learned and practiced outdoor survival skills. At night, away from city lights, we could easily see the stars and the Milky Way. At the end of our campfire programs, we sang the first two verses of "How Great Thou Art" which was "written by Carl Gustav Boberg in Sweden in 1885 … following a two mile walk through a thunderstorm from a church meeting" (http://en.wikipedia.org/wiki/How_Great_Thou_Art_(hymn)).

    How Great Thou Art, English trans. Stuart K. Hine

1. O Lord my God! When I in awesome wonder
   Consider all the works Thy hands have made.
   I see the stars, I hear the rolling thunder,
   Thy power through-out the universe displayed.

2. When through the woods and forest glades I wander
   And hear the birds sing sweetly in the trees;
   When I look down from lofty mountain grandeur
   And hear the brook and feel the gentle breeze:

Chorus:
   Then sings my soul, my Savior God, to Thee;
   How great Thou art, how great Thou art!

We reminded scouts that "the earth, and all things that are upon the face of it, yea, and its motion, yea, and also all the planets which move in their regular form do witness that there is a Supreme Creator" (Alma 30:44). The Lord said "all things are created and made to bear record of me …; things which are in the heavens above, …

on the earth, ... in the earth, and ... under the earth" (Moses 6:63). That which bears record of the Lord reminds us of Him. Unfortunately, it is not always easy to understand how *all* things "bear record" of the Lord.

Over the years I have realized that many things we saw and did in the outdoors were used as symbols in the scriptures. The things we see and do in the outdoors can be mnemonics to help us remember Christ and his teachings during the year. Understanding the meanings of nature symbols can help us understand the scriptures.

The remainder of this book is a discussion of twenty-four earthly and heavenly symbols that remind me of Christ. Each picture has a brief explanation that is followed by some other ideas and scriptures that relate Christ to the symbol. Old Testament scriptures refer to Jehovah, the God of the Old Testament, who would come down among the children of men, ... redeem his people" and dwell in the flesh as Jesus Christ (*BD*, s.v. "Jehovah"). The Hebrew word for Jehovah (YHWH) is translated as LORD in the King James Bible.

Each picture or a related object (e.g., rock) could be used as an advent ornament with a brief explanation. You may want to read the short explanation of all of the pictures first, and then read the additional information about each symbol.

1. Wilderness

Wilderness Trail

Summary: As Jehovah, Christ sent Lehi's family to wilderness school for eight years, where they experienced hunger, thirst, and danger. Christ guided, protected, provided for, and revealed himself to them when they trusted in him. Jesus went to the wilderness to be with God and fast. There he taught and fed 5,000 with five loaves and two fishes (Matt. 14:13–21).

Scout outings are often in what we call a wilderness. Like Nephi, scouts prepare for outings, leave home, and go into a "wilderness school" where they practice living the Scout Law (e.g., trustworthy, loyal, helpful, obedient, cheerful). Many feel like home is a Garden of Eden or Promised Land compared to the wilderness where they see wild animals, sleep in a tent, start fires, cook meals, purify drinking water, and get wet or cold.

In the Bible and 1 Nephi, *wilderness* almost always means desert.

Judean Wilderness © D. Kelly Ogden

As Jehovah or LORD, Christ delivered Moses and the Israelites out of Egypt and sent them to wilderness school for 40 years before they entered the Promised Land. Even though they had seen miracles in Egypt, at the Red Sea, and in the wilderness (e.g., manna, water), they still murmured or complained about their circumstances. They learned gratitude and obedience by the things they suffered. Christ gave Moses instructions regarding the Day of Atonement when a scapegoat carried the sins of the people into the wilderness and died.

John the Baptist preached in the wilderness and baptized in the river Jordan. Jesus was led by the Spirit "into the wilderness to be with God" (JST Matt. 4:1). There he "was with the wild beasts" (Mark 1:13), and after 40 days Satan tempted him (JST Luke 4:1–2). In

Christ's parable of the Good Samaritan, a man travels from Jerusalem to Jericho through the wilderness where lone travelers were easy prey (Luke 10:25–37). In his parable of the lost sheep, the shepherd leaves "the ninety and nine in the wilderness" to go after a lost sheep (Luke 15:4). The JST says the shepherd leaves the ninety and nine to "go into the wilderness after that which is lost" (JST Luke 15:4).

If people "keep the commandments of God he doth nourish them, and strengthen them, and provide means whereby they can accomplish the thing which he has commanded them; wherefore, he did provide means for us while we did sojourn in the wilderness … [for] eight years" (1 Ne. 17:2–4).

After the crucifixion, the Church fled into the wilderness (JST Rev. 12:1–7; D&C 86:3). In the last days the Church was "called forth out of the wilderness" (D&C 33:5). The priesthood was restored in the wilderness (D&C 128:20).

2. Mountains

Provo Utah Temple near Squaw Peak

> **Summary:** Mountains are nature's temples. As Jehovah, Christ told his prophets to go up into mountains where he talked with them face to face. Jesus went into mountains to pray. The garden of Gethsemane is on the Mount of Olives. In the mount of transfiguration, Peter, James, and John saw Moses and Elijah appear to the transfigured Jesus. Temples are often built on or near mountains and point heavenward like mountains. Temples are places of prayer and revelation.

Scouts often go to the mountains for outings and scout camps where they enjoy backpacking, fishing, hiking, and camping. They often see birds, land animals, fish, trees, and plants.

As Jehovah, Christ talked with Adam in the Garden of Eden, which was on a mountain where a river began and flowed downward (Parry, 133–137). Christ told Abraham to take Isaac to Mount Moriah to be sacrificed, provided a ram as a substitute, and blessed Abraham (Gen. 22). Later, Solomon built the temple on Mount Moriah, where the LORD had appeared to King David (2 Chr. 3:1). Christ was crucified on Mount Moriah. Christ told Enoch to go up on a mount, where he beheld the heavens open, and he saw and talked with the Christ (Moses 7:2–4). Christ talked with Moses several times on Mount Sinai. Christ gave Moses the Ten Commandments, spoke with Moses face to face (Ex. 33:11), told him how to make the tabernacle (moveable temple), and revealed the temple ordinances to him. On a high mountain, Moses saw Christ face to face and was shown the creation of the world (Moses 1:1–2; 2). Christ appeared to the Brother of Jared on a high mountain (Ether 3:1–16). Christ told Nephi to go into a mountain where he showed Nephi how to build a ship (1 Ne. 17:7–14). Nephi went into the mountain often to pray, and Christ showed him great things (1 Ne. 18:3).

Jesus "went up into a mountain apart to pray" after teaching the multitudes (Matt. 14:23). Before choosing his apostles, Jesus "went out into a mountain to pray, and continued all night in prayer to God" (Luke 6:12). Jesus took Peter, James, and John into a high mountain where they saw Moses and Elijah appear to a transfigured Jesus (Matt. 17:1–9). Before his crucifixion, Jesus went to pray in Gethsemane on the Mount of Olives.

Isaiah prophesied that "in the last days, when the mountain of the Lord's house shall be established in the top of the mountains, ... many people shall go and say, Come ye, and let us go up to the mountain of the Lord, to the house of the God of Jacob; and he will teach us of his ways, and we will walk in his paths" (2 Ne. 12:3).

3. Rocks and Stone

Rock Canyon

Summary: As Jehovah, Christ wrote the Ten Commandments on stone tablets and made water come out of a rock. He is the Rock. Jesus was laid in a stone manger at birth and buried in a tomb cut out of rock. He is the chief cornerstone of the church, and the Book of Mormon is the keystone of our religion.

Scouts often throw and climb rocks. Rocks can be used for weapons, snares, tools, fire starters, cooking surfaces, tent supports, shelter, warmth, etc.

As Jehovah, Christ touched sixteen small stones to provide light for the Brother of Jared as they crossed the ocean (Ether 3:1–6). Jacob placed a stone pillar at Beth-el, or *house of God*, where Christ appeared to him in a dream (Gen. 28:10–22). Christ wrote the Ten Commandments on stone tablets (Ex. 24:12). Christ told Moses to engrave the names of the tribes on two stones to be on the shoulders of the high priest's ephod (Ex. 28:9–12). Christ told Moses to smite a rock, and drinking water came out of it (Ex. 17:6). Christ was called the Rock (Deut. 32:4; 1 Cor. 10:4) and stone of Israel (Gen. 49:24). Christ commanded Moses to make an altar of stone (Ex. 20:25). By means of David and five stones, Christ delivered the Israelites from Goliath and the Philistines (1 Sam. 17:47–50). The temple of Solomon was built of stone and wood (1 Kgs. 6). Stone walls surrounded the temple and Jerusalem.

Teachings of Jesus: Those who follow his teachings are like a man who built his house on a rock to withstand the storms (Matt. 7:24). Seeds that fall on a rock will spring up and die for lack of water. Likewise, some people receive the word with joy but quickly fall away when tempted or tried (Luke 8:6, 13). Jesus said, "thou art Peter (GR: small rock), and upon this rock (GR: bedrock) I will build my church; and the gates of hell shall not prevail against it" (Matt. 16:18). This *rock* has been interpreted as Peter, love, revelation, or the gospel.[9]

Jesus probably was born in a rock cave, was laid in a stone manger, lived in a stone house, and became a stone craftsman. In Palestine, trees were scarce. On the plains,

---

[9] Catholic leaders say the church would be built on *Peter*. Some oriental Christians say that "Christ would build His Church on the rock-bed of ***love***. If I wanted to say…, 'I love you,' I would say, 'I love you as a rock in the rock-bed.' In Jerusalem, in the Mosque of Omar, where the holy rock is, we… [say] 'In this rock-bed of thy love will I build My Church'" (Mountford 1911, 185–186). Joseph Smith said the church would be built on the rock of *revelation* (*TPJS*, 274 or 282). After teaching about faith, repentance, baptism, and the Holy Ghost (a source of revelation), Christ said "this is my *doctrine*, and whoso buildeth upon this buildeth upon my rock, and the gates of hell shall not prevail against them" (3 Ne. 11:34). "Build upon my rock, which is my *gospel*" (D&C 11:24; 33:13). Jesus said this is "my gospel": (a) I came to do the will of the Father, be lifted up on the cross, and judge all people, and (b) those who have faith, repent, are baptized, receive the Holy Ghost, and endure to the end will be saved (3 Ne. 27:13–21).

where stone is rare, houses are made of sun-dried brick, but in the mountains they are built of stone except for a wooden door. (Whiting 1929, 719, 727; 1914, 249, 251, 310; 1926, 736). Τέκτον, the Greek word for *carpenter* (Mark 6:3), means "artificer" or "craftsman." In the Greek Old Testament or Septuagint (LXX) this word often was used to translate the Hebrew word *chārāsh*, which means an artificer or craftsman who works with metal, wood, or stone (*BDB*). Joseph and Jesus may have been "craftsmen of stone, which was much more available and used in the building trades" (Ogden and Skinner, 300; Rona 2001a, 38).

Jesus changed the water in stone waterpots into wine (John 2:6). The Jews tried to stone Jesus (John 10:31). Jesus had the stone removed from a cave and raised Lazarus from the dead (John 11:38–44). When Christ died, the earth quaked and the rocks broke in two (Matt. 27:51; 3 Ne. 8:18). Christ was buried in a new tomb cut out of rock and a great stone as a door (Matt. 27:60). The church of Jesus Christ is "built upon the foundation of the apostles and prophets, Jesus Christ himself being the chief corner stone" (Eph. 2:20). To those who enter the celestial kingdom, Christ will give a white stone with a new name written on it that will become a Urim and Thummim (D&C 130:10–11; Rev. 2:17).

Joseph Smith found the gold plates buried in a stone box (JS—H 1:51). After a meeting with the Council of Twelve Apostles on Sunday, Nov. 28, 1841, Joseph Smith wrote, "I told the brethren that the Book of Mormon was the most correct of any book on earth, and the *keystone* of our religion, and a man would get nearer to God by abiding by its precepts, than by any other book" (*HC* 4:461; italics added).

4. Rivers

Provo River at Canyon Glen

Summary: As Jehovah, Christ provided living water for his creations. Jesus was baptized in the river that cured Naaman of leprosy. Joseph Smith received the Aaronic and Melchizedek Priesthoods on the banks of a river and was baptized in it.

Scouts often develop a new appreciation for water when it is not available to them from a tap. They may need to find, carry and purify it since without water, a person will die in a few days. They also learn to recognize and treat dehydration.

As Jehovah, Christ planted a garden in Eden, and a river (living water) flowed downward from there to the four parts of the world (Gen. 2:8–14. Parry, 133–137). Christ protected the baby Moses who was put in an ark, or basket, and floated in the river Nile to avoid being killed (Ex. 2:3). Christ had Moses turn the river Nile to blood and cause frogs to come out of the river (Ex. 7:19; 8:5). In the desert, Christ helped them find water, made bitter water sweet, and made water come out of a rock (Ex. 15:22–27; 17:6). Christ helped Joshua and the Israelites cross the river Jordan on dry ground (Josh. 3:8–17) just as he had helped Moses and the Israelites cross the Red Sea (Ex. 15:4–19). Christ's prophets, Elijah and Elisha, smote the river Jordan and crossed on dry ground (2 Kgs. 2:8, 14). Elisha told Naaman to wash in the river Jordan seven times to be cured of leprosy (2 Kgs. 5:2).

Jesus and others were baptized by John the Baptist in the river Jordan (Matt. 3:6–13; Mark 1:5–11; Luke 3:21). The river of living or moving water was a source of life to plants, trees, animals, and people. Jesus said, "He that believeth on me, as the scripture hath said, out of his belly shall flow rivers of living water" (John 7:38). In the last days, rivers will turn to blood and dry up to destroy the wicked (Rev. 16:4, 12).

Lehi camped near a river of water that he called Laman (1 Ne. 2:6–8). A river of filthiness was near the tree and the rod in Lehi's dream (1 Ne. 15:26).

On the banks of Susquehanna River in Harmony, Pennsylvania, John the Baptist appeared to Joseph Smith and Oliver Cowdery on 15 May 1829 (JS—H 1:66–74; D&C 13) and conferred the Aaronic Priesthood on them. Then they baptized each other in this river. Sometime later, Peter, James, and John appeared on the banks of this river and conferred on Joseph and Oliver the Melchizedek Priesthood (D&C 27:12–13; 128:20).

Isaiah prophesied that in the last days, the wilderness or desert would blossom as the rose (Isa. 35:1, 7). "I [Christ] will open rivers in high places, and fountains in the midst of the valleys: I will make the wilderness a pool of water, and the dry land springs of water" (Isa. 41:18). The Salt Lake valley was a desert when the pioneers arrived and now has blossomed like a rose.

5. Fish and Fishing

Fishermen on the Sea of Galilee © D. Kelly Ogden

Summary: As Jehovah, Christ created sea creatures and told Moses that some were good to eat while others were not. Jesus fed 5,000 in the wilderness with some bread and two fishes. He invited fishermen to become fishers of men. He ate fish after his resurrection to show his apostles he was not a spirit.

Scouts enjoy fishing on a lake or by a river. They learn how to catch fish with lures and bait, and how to clean and cook fish. Scouts are taught that conspiring men use enticing bait to get them to smoke, drink, take drugs, and sin. Once hooked, they are no longer free and may lie, steal, die, or kill.

As Jehovah, Christ created whales and other sea creatures (Gen. 1:21). He told Moses that fish with fins and scales were clean or good to eat, but others (e.g., catfish, shrimp, lobster, shark, dolphin) were unclean. Christ prepared a great fish to swallow up Jonah" for "three days and three nights" (Jonah 1:17) as a sign of how long he would be in the grave (Matt. 12:39). He said he would gather the lost tribes by sending many fishers to fish them (Jer. 16:14–16).

In a desert wilderness, Jesus fed 5,000 men with five loaves of bread and two fishes (Matt. 14:13–21; Mark 6:30–44; Luke 9:1–11). He also fed 4,000 with seven loaves of bread and a few fishes (Matt. 15:32–39). Jesus paid his tribute, or tax, with a coin Peter found in the mouth of the first fish he caught (Matt. 17:24–27).

Jesus said to his apostles, "Follow me, and I will make you fishers of men" (Matt. 4:18–19; Mark 1:1–17). He also said "the kingdom of heaven is like unto a net, that was cast into the sea, and gathered of every kind: Which, when it was full, they drew to shore, ... and gathered the good into vessels, but cast the bad away" (Matt. 13:47–48). "Fish are symbols of men (Hab. 1:14; Eccl. 9:12). The law of Moses declared some fish clean and others unclean (Lev. 11:9–12; Deut. 14:9–10). So also are the children of men" (McConkie and Parry, 51).

After his resurrection, Jesus appeared to the apostles in Jerusalem. To show them he was not a spirit, Jesus let them touch his hands and feet. Then he ate some fish (Luke 24:36–43). Later, Jesus saw his apostles fishing and told them to cast their net on the other side of the ship. They did so and caught a multitude of fishes. Jesus ate bread and fish with them (John 21:1–14).

The ancient Greek word for fish, ΙΧΘΥΣ (IChThYS) became an acronym for Ἰησοῦς Χριστός, Θεοῦ Υἱός, Σωτήρ (Jesus Christ, Son of God, Savior). The fish symbol became associated with early Christians who used it as a sign with a secret meaning unknown to their Roman persecutors (Withrow, 252).

6. Trees and Plants

Gethsemane Grove © Derek J. Hegsted

Summary: As Jehovah, Christ created trees and other plants to beautify the earth and to provide food, clothing, and shelter. He put Adam and Eve in the Garden of Eden. Jesus is the Bread of Life and the True Vine. Christ prayed and suffered in the Garden of Gethsemane. Christ appeared to Joseph Smith in a grove of trees near his home. Joseph received the priesthood among trees and plants on the banks of a river.

Trees provide scouts with shade and shelter and with wood for fires, tools, weapons, and shelter. Some plants are edible, some are beautiful, and some are to be avoided (e.g., thorns, thistles, poison oak or poison ivy).

As Jehovah, Christ created trees and other plants "for food or for raiment, or for houses, or for barns, or for orchards, or for gardens, or for vineyards; Yea, all things which come of the earth, in the season thereof, are made for the benefit and the use of man, both to please the eye and to gladden the heart; Yea, for food and for raiment, for taste and for smell, to strengthen the body and to enliven the soul" (D&C 59:16–20). Nephites generally did not die of fevers "because of the excellent qualities of the many plants and roots which God had prepared to remove the cause of diseases, to which men were subject by the nature of the climate" (Alma 46:40). Christ told Moses to use several plant products (e.g., frankincense, bread, wine, first fruits) in the tabernacle. All plant food was considered "clean." In Solomon's temple, the holy place represented the Garden of Eden. Figures of plants (e.g., palm trees, flowers) were carved in the walls (1 Kgs. 6:29, 32, 35). The menorah represented the Tree of Life, and cherubim were on the veil (Parry, 129, 135, 139).

Jesus was born in Bethlehem (HEB: house of bread). He is the Bread of Life and the True Vine (John 6:35; 15:1). At the last supper, Jesus blessed bread and wine and told the apostles to eat and drink in remembrance of him (Luke 22:18–20). Jesus was called the Good Shepherd. A shepherd used a wooden staff and a club (or rod) to guide and defend his sheep.

Christ and his servants often used the familiar characteristics of plants (e.g., mustard seed) to teach spiritual lessons. "Every good tree bringeth forth good fruit; but a corrupt tree bringeth forth evil fruit. …

Wherefore, by their fruits ye shall know them" (3 Ne. 14:16–20). "He ... that received seed among the thorns is he that heareth the word; and the care of this world, and the deceitfulness of riches, choke the word, and he becometh unfruitful" (Matt. 13:22). Faith is like a seed that must be nourished to grow (Alma 32). "Whatsoever a man soweth, that shall he also reap" (Gal. 6:7). A man's enemy planted tares among the wheat (Matt. 13:25–30; D&C 86:1–7).

God, the Father, and Christ appeared to Joseph Smith in the Sacred Grove near his home in Palmyra, New York (JS—H 1:14–20). Christ revealed to Joseph the sacrament prayers for the bread and wine (D&C 20:77–79).

7. Animals

Birds, land animals, creeping things, and insects

> **Summary:** As Jehovah, Christ created the birds, land animals, and everything that creeps upon the earth. He ordained the beasts of the field, birds, and plants "for the use of man for food and for raiment" (D&C 49:19).

Scouts enjoy watching wild animals and birds. The eagle represents freedom. It is the national bird of the United States and the name of the highest scouting award.

As Jehovah, Christ made coats of animal skins for Adam and Eve (Gen. 3:21) and commanded them to offer animal sacrifices (Moses 5:6). He commanded the Israelites to eat roasted lamb for Passover each year (Ex. 12:3–14). The priests ate parts of animal sacrifices and used the animal skins (Lev. 7:5–9). Nephi used a bow and arrow to kill wild beasts for food (1 Ne. 16:31). Enos hunted beasts in the forest (Enos 1:3).

Christ told Moses which animals were clean and could be eaten and which were unclean and could not be eaten (Lev. 11; Deut. 14). They could slaughter animals in their towns if the temple was far away, but they should not eat the blood of animals (Deut. 12:20–24). If they ate meat from an animal found dead without the blood being drained, they were unclean until evening and must wash their clothes and bathe (Lev. 17:15; Deut. 14:21). Idol worship often included drinking blood or eating unclean animals. These practices were not part of worshiping God and made a person unclean or unworthy to go to the temple until the next day, after they had bathed.

Birds of prey (e.g., eagle, owl, raven) were unclean, but other birds were clean. With the exception of locusts, flying insects (e.g., flies, bees) were unclean. Creeping things (e.g., snakes, lizards, mice, squirrels) were unclean. Animals with a cloven hoof that chew their cud were clean. These include cow, goat, sheep, deer, antelope, moose, pronghorn, and giraffe. Unclean animals included rabbit, pig, camel, donkey, and animals with paws or claws, such as lion, bear, wolf, and monkey (Lev. 11; Deut. 14). Many unclean animals eat other animals. Jesus allowed devils to enter unclean swine and the whole herd drowned (Matt. 8:31–33).

In the millennium, meat eating animals (e.g., wolf, leopard, lion, bear) will dwell with plant eating animals (e.g., lamb, goat, calf) and will also eat plant food (2 Ne. 21:6–8; Isa. 11:6–8). Meat eating animals also ate plant food in the Garden of Eden (Gen. 1:30). In the Bible, "meat" means food in general not the flesh of animals.

When Jesus was baptized, "the Holy Ghost descended upon him in the form of a dove, and sat upon him" (D&C

93:15; John 1:32). Jews eat roasted lamb at Passover. When the prodigal son returned, his father killed the fatted calf for a meal (Luke 15:23).

Early gentile Christians were to "abstain from meats offered to idols, and from blood, and from things strangled" (Acts 15:29). Christ said that a person who forbids people to eat meat "is not ordained of God; For, behold, the beasts of the field and the fowls of the air, and that which cometh of the earth, is ordained for the use of man for food and for raiment" (D&C 49:18–19). However, he also says, "Wo be unto man that sheddeth blood or that wasteth flesh and hath no need" (D&C 49:21). The Word of Wisdom says, "flesh also of beasts and of the fowls of the air, I, the Lord, have ordained for the use of man with thanksgiving; nevertheless they are to be used sparingly; And it is pleasing unto me that they should not be used, only in times of winter, or of cold, or famine" (D&C 89:10–13; Gen. 9:3; see JST Gen. 9:4).

8. Fire

Campfire, photo by Dirk Beyer

Summary: As Jehovah, Christ appeared to Moses in a flame of fire and guided the Israelites in a pillar of fire by night. Christ uses fire to purify the righteous and to destroy the wicked. He invites all to be baptized by water and by fire and the Holy Ghost.

Scouts learn how to start, care for, cook on, and properly put out a fire. Where allowed, a campfire at night is a fun part of outings. Fire provides light to see in the dark. Fire gives off heat for cooking and for getting warm. For the metalwork merit badge, they learn that fire is used to refine and work with metal. Fire can also destroy forests, cities, and living things.

As Jehovah, Christ placed a flaming sword to guard the tree of life (Alma 42:2). Christ appeared to Moses "in a flame of fire" and a burning bush (Ex. 3:2; 19:18). When Moses brought the people "to meet with God," Christ descended on Mount Sinai "in fire" (Ex. 19:17–18). When Moses came down the mountain with the Ten Commandments, the mount burned with fire (Deut. 9:15). In a cloud by day and a pillar of fire by night, Christ guided the Israelites (Ex. 13:21; Num. 9:15–16). In the temple, fire was continually on the altar of sacrifice, on the altar of incense where the rising smoke represented prayers rising to heaven, and on the menorah or lampstand to light the holy place continually (Lev. 6:3; Rev. 8:4; Lev. 24:2). Christ sent down fire from heaven to destroy the wicked (Gen. 19:24; Lev. 10:2; Num. 11:1; 16:35; 2 Kgs. 1:10–14; Amos 1:4–14; 2:2) and to burn the sacrifices of Moses, Elijah, David, and Solomon (Lev. 9:24; 1 Kgs. 18:38; 1 Chr. 21:26; 2 Chr. 7:1).

Jesus cooked fish and bread on a fire, fed his apostles, and then asked Peter to feed his sheep (John 21:9–15). He said, "every tree that bringeth not forth good fruit is ... cast into the fire" (Matt. 7:19) and the tares will be burned with fire (Matt. 13:40). When Christ was crucified, wicked Nephite cities were burned with fire (3 Ne. 9:3, 9, 10). Christ said, "whoso cometh unto me ..., him will I baptize with fire and with the Holy Ghost, even as the Lamanites ... and they knew it not" (3 Ne. 9:20). Melchizedek priesthood holders have authority "to confirm those who are baptized ... by the laying on of hands for the baptism of fire and the Holy Ghost" (D&C 20:41).

At his second coming, Christ will come "in a pillar of fire" and will say to the wicked, "Depart from me, ye cursed, into everlasting fire, prepared for the devil and his angels" (D&C 29:10–12, 27–28). Christ "is like a refiner's fire ... and he shall sit as a refiner and purifier of silver, and he shall purify the sons of Levi, and purge them as gold and silver, that they may offer unto the Lord an offering in righteousness" (D&C 128:24; Rev. 9:18). "Fire represents God's desire to destroy sin and to purify his people (cf. Isa. 6:6–7)" (*DBI*, s.v. "Fire"). "God Almighty … dwells in eternal fire; flesh and blood cannot go there, for all corruption is devoured by the fire" (*TPJS*, 367 or 380). "Angels do not reside on a planet like this earth; But they reside in the presence of God, on a globe like a sea of glass and fire" (D&C 130:6–7). Christ's "eyes were as a flame of fire" (Rev. 1:14; 2:18; D&C 110:3).

9. Storms

Mountain Lightening Storm © Peter McIntosh

Summary: Christ uses storms and drought to destroy the wicked and to bless and humble people. He prepares a way for his people to survive both storms and drought. He said, "If ye are prepared ye shall not fear" (D&C 38:30).

During campouts, scouts become familiar with storms. The wind may shake or flatten their tents. The boys may get wet and cold. A few boys have died in flash floods or when struck by lightning. Lightning may start a forest fire. Scouts learn to be prepared and to take precautions during storms. Storms may bring danger and death, but they also cleanse the earth and bring the water necessary for new life.

As Jehovah, Christ commanded Noah to build an ark and then caused it to rain for 40 days (Gen. 7:4). He rained hail on Egypt (Ex. 9:23). He said, "If ye ... keep my commandments, ... then I will give you rain in due season" for good harvests (Lev. 26:4). He shuts the heavens when people ripen in iniquity and prepares a way for the righteous to survive (Gen. 12:5; Gen. 41:54; 45:6–7; 1 Kgs. 17:1; Hel. 11:4–5; Ether 9:30).

Jesus sends life-giving "rain on the just and on the unjust" (Matt. 5:45). On a ship during a storm, Jesus calmed the sea for his frightened disciples (Matt. 8:24–27; 14:24–32). Sometimes he calms the hearts of his people and helps them prepare for and deal with storms. He invited disciples to build their houses on a rock that would withstand the rain, floods, and wind (Matt. 7:25). When Jesus died, there was a great storm and earthquake (3 Ne. 8:6–19; Matt. 27:51–54).

Christ uses storms to bless and humble his people. He prepared the brother of Jared for storms that would drive his people to the promised land (Ether 12:25). Wind propelled the ship carrying Lehi's family to the promised land. When Laman and Lemuel forgot God, bound Nephi, and treated him harshly, a great storm arose. "Nothing save it were the power of God, which threatened them with destruction, could soften their hearts" (1 Ne. 18:8–20). "As they were unfaithful they did not prosper nor progress in their journey, but were driven back, and incurred the displeasure of God upon them; and therefore they were smitten with famine and sore afflictions, to stir them up in remembrance of their duty" to love God and neighbor (Mosiah 1:17). "Except the Lord doth chasten his people with many afflictions, yea, except he doth visit them with death and with terror, and with famine and with all manner of pestilence, they will not remember him" (Hel. 12:3).

When a storm is coming, a hen gathers her chicks under her wings to protect them. Christ said, "How often would I have gathered you together as a hen gathereth her chickens under her wings, but ye would not! How oft have I called upon you by the mouth of my servants, … [my] angels, and by mine own voice, and by the voice of thunderings, … lightnings, … tempests, … earthquakes, … hailstorms, and … famines and pestilences of every kind" (D&C 43:24–25).

10. Travel

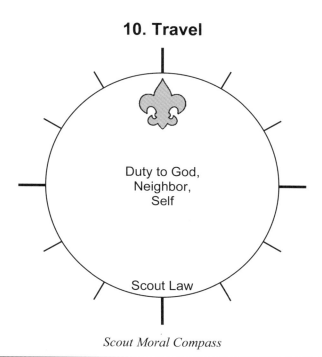

Scout Moral Compass

Summary: Christ guided the Israelites and Lehi's family in the wilderness for many years. He invites us to receive the Holy Ghost to guide us in wisdom's paths that we may be blessed, prospered, and preserved.

The trefoil (⚜) is like the north point of the compasses that were used for many years to guide sailors. The three points stand for the three parts of the Scout Oath, which should guide scouts in life: duty (a) to God and country, (b) to other people, and (c) to themselves. The Scout Law has 12 points, represented by the lines in the above diagram. These 12 points are: trustworthy, loyal, helpful, friendly, courteous, kind, obedient, cheerful, thrifty, brave, clean, and reverent. The Scout Oath and Law are a scout's moral compass.

Scouts learn to use a map, a compass, and the North Star to know where they are and the direction they want to go. However, in the wilderness it is sometimes difficult to be sure where you are and to know the best way to get to your destination. Today, GPS devices can more accurately help people know where they are and how to get to their destination. GPS navigation systems for cars act as a guide and tell the driver when to turn and when they arrive at their destination.

As Jehovah, Christ went before the Israelites "by day in a pillar of a cloud, to lead them the way; and by night in a pillar of fire, to give them light" (Ex. 13:21; Num. 9:15–16). Christ guided Lehi's family in the wilderness with a Liahona, or ball. This "compass" pointed the way they should go and led them "in the more fertile parts of the wilderness." Sometimes words appeared on the ball (1 Ne. 16:10, 16, 25–28). It worked "according to their faith in God" (Alma 37:37–46). Such a guide would be more effective than a map and compass! A map helps a scout know his location and where other things are located, but it does not tell the scout where to go or the best way to get there. Similarly, young Joseph Smith understood the beliefs of various churches but prayed for wisdom, "for how to act I did not know" (JS—H 1:12).

Christ has invited all to be baptized and receive the Holy Ghost "to guide you in wisdom's paths that ye may be blessed, prospered, and preserved" (Mosiah 2:36; Hel. 12:6; D&C 45:57).

In the scriptures, east is considered to be the sacred direction. The door to ancient temples faced east. At his second coming, Christ will come from the east (JS—M 1:26; Matt. 24:27).

11. Survival

The Good Samaritan by Walter Rane © Intellectual Reserve, Inc.

Summary: Christ came to earth to heal the sick, afflicted, blind, deaf and dumb. He gave his disciples the authority and responsibility to do the same (James 5:14–15; Mosiah 3:5; 3 Ne. 7:32; 26:15; 4 Ne. 1:1; D&C 24:13; 35:9; 84:66–73; 124:98–100). Christ is the Good Samaritan who cares for each of us who are wounded physically or spiritually. He invites us to love our neighbors by helping others who need physical or spiritual help (Luke 10:25–36).

In the wilderness, people can die from lack of air, water, and food; from bleeding, animal bites, injury, infection, or sickness; from bad food or water; from inadequate clothing and shelter, resulting in hypothermia or heatstroke; and from flash floods, lightning, accidents, and wild animal attacks. Scouts promise "to help other people at all times," and the Scout Motto is "Be Prepared." All scouts are expected to learn first aid to handle life-threatening situations, to protect an injured or ill person from further harm, and to get medical help for the victim. Special awards are given to scouts who save a life. Scouts also learn principles of health and safety to help prevent sickness, injury, and death. Scouts use the buddy system to help each other.

When Lehi took his family into the wilderness, Nephi was prepared spiritually and physically. He took a bow and knew how to make a new bow. He knew how to hunt wild beasts for food. He made fire by striking two stones together, and he made tools from metal ore. He received revelation from Christ to make a ship, avoid robbers, and solve other problems. (See 1 Ne. 16:31–32; 17:7–12.)

In the last days, there will be earthquakes, thunder, lightning, tempests, and flooding, and "fear shall come upon all people" (D&C 88:91), but Christ promises that "if ye are prepared ye shall not fear" (D&C 38:30). Latter-day prophets encourage us to have a supply of drinking water, a year's supply of food, and first aid kits so that we will be prepared to take care of ourselves and to help others during emergencies.

We might see ourselves as *the Good Samaritan* and help people physically or spiritually as saviors on Mount Zion. Good Samaritan laws exist to protect people who try to help sick or injured people until medical help can arrive. "Remember in all things the poor and the needy, the sick and the afflicted, for he that doeth not these things ... is not my disciple" (D&C 52:40). We might also see ourselves as *innkeepers* in the church who have been commissioned by the Good Samaritan (Christ) to help with the spiritual recovery of injured travelers. Or we might see ourselves as the *traveler* wounded by sin in this telestial world, helped by the Good Samaritan (Christ), who will return in glory, and nourished by the innkeeper who represents church leaders (Welch, 40–47).

12. Sun, Moon, Stars

Sunset in Israel   Moon, Venus and Stars

Summary: Christ created the sun, moon, and stars for signs, seasons, days, and years (Gen. 1:14–18; Moses 2:14–16). He makes "his sun rise on the evil and on the good" (Matt. 5:45).

In the outdoors, scouts learn to appreciate the sun's warmth and light and the beauty of the night sky. They learn to use the location of the sun, moon, and stars to determine direction and time.

As Jehovah, Christ said, "all things are created and made to bear record of me ... things which are in the heavens above" and things which are on, in, and under the earth (Moses 6:63).

As discussed with the nativity stories, Jesus died and was probably born at Passover, which was always during a full moon. A star guided the wise men to baby Jesus, (Matt. 2:2, 9) and Nephites saw a new star (3 Ne. 1:21). When Jesus was transfigured, "his face did shine as the sun" (Matt. 17:2). When Jesus died, people saw no light from the sun, moon, stars, or fire (3 Ne. 8:22). Women saw his empty tomb Sunday morning at sunrise (Luke 24:1–7).

When Paul talked with the resurrected Christ, he saw a "light from heaven above the brightness of the sun" (Acts 26:12). Joseph Smith said, "I saw a pillar of light ..., above the brightness of the sun ... [and] I saw [God, the Father, and Jesus Christ], whose brightness and glory defy all description" (JS—H 1:16–17). When Joseph and Oliver saw Christ, "his countenance shone above the brightness of the sun" (D&C 110:3). Jesus called himself "the bright and morning star" or Venus (Rev. 22:16).

Before the second coming, "there shall be signs in the sun, and in the moon, and in the stars" (Luke 21:25). "The sun shall be darkened, and the moon be turned into blood, and the stars fall from heaven" (D&C 45:42; 29:14; Acts 2:20). The phrase "moon turned to blood" has been used since 300 BC to describe lunar eclipses because the moon appears red during total and some partial eclipses (Humphreys and Waddington, 172–177).

Christ compared the glory of the celestial kingdom to the sun, the terrestrial to the moon, and the telestial to the stars (D&C 76:96–98; 1 Cor. 15:41).

Alma compared faith to a seed that must be nourished to get root, grow, and bear fruit. The same sun that causes plants with root to grow also causes plants with no root to wither and die (Alma 32:38; Matt. 13:4–8).

Alma said "all things denote there is a God; yea, even the earth, and all things that are upon the face of it, yea, and its motion, yea, and also all the planets which move in their regular form do witness that there is a Supreme Creator" (Alma 30:44).

Constellation Ornaments

To become a first class scout a boy must know how to find the Big Dipper and the North Star. On our campouts we used a star chart to find other constellations and noticed how they rotated around the North Star. "For thousands of years, people have imagined they could see groups of stars forming the shapes of warriors, animals, maidens, and monsters. Many of the names they gave these constellations are still with us today" (*The Boy Scout Handbook*, 11th ed., 114). Many people are aware of the names of the twelve constellations of the Zodiac (e.g., Aquarius, Capricorn, Gemini, Virgo) through which the sun, moon, and planets all appear to move.

> Traditionally there were 48 constellations ...: 12 principal constellations in a circle around the entire sky called the zodiac, with three other constellations ... which accompanied each of those twelve. Generally there is good agreement between ancient nations on just what those 48 are, but there have been minor disagreements on three or four of them. (Pratt 2005)

Books about the constellations often tell the pagan constellation stories about the adventures of Greek gods and heroes. However, in 1865 a Christian scholar proposed that the constellations originally were given by God to bear record of the coming of the Messiah, His atonement, and His second coming. Later writers popularized this theory. An LDS astronomer reviewed the theory, its strengths, its weaknesses, and answered objections (Pratt 2004). The constellations of the Persians, Egyptians, and Greeks may have been revealed originally to Enoch, Abraham, and other prophets.

> The Book of Enoch declares that an angel revealed to Enoch how to draw the constellations and scientific research confirms

that the figures are old enough for that to be true. ... Nearly all ancient nations, including the Greeks, Romans and Egyptians, attributed the constellations to a divine source. The Hebrews, Persians and Arabs attributed them to the antediluvian patriarchs such as Adam, Seth and Enoch. Modern astronomy confirms that the figures most likely originated about 2900 B.C., which is approximately when Enoch lived. Abraham, who was born nearly a thousand years later, tells us that he had records of the patriarchs with knowledge of the stars, and that he had much astronomy revealed to him personally. He... was commanded to teach astronomy to the Egyptians (Abr. 1:31; 3:1–15), who reportedly passed the knowledge of the constellations on to the Greeks, who recorded it for us. (Pratt 2001)

Scholars debate the history of constellations and what they symbolized based on star names or myths. However, I can personally choose what I want to remember when I see them or hear their names. Just as someone might tie a string around his finger to remind him of what to do, I can tie a mental string around the constellations to remind myself of Christ instead of Greek myths. When I see a constellation or discuss someone's sign, I can use this mental string to remember Christ.

The last twelve advent ornaments are the twelve zodiac constellations, each with three nearby constellations that remind me of Christ's different titles or roles. After a brief explanation, additional information is provided. My groupings and explanations differ somewhat from those proposed by others. All constellation images are courtesy of John P. Pratt. Italics have been added to keywords in scripture quotations that refer to the constellations.

Since the birth of Jesus marks the beginning of his mortal life, we start with the Maiden or Virgo which relates to the birth of an infant prince (Christ). Interestingly *Rosh Hashanah*, the Jewish New Year (1

Tishri) or the first day of the civil year, usually occurs between August 23rd and September 22nd while the sun is in this constellation. According to Jewish tradition, God created Adam and Eve on this day (http://en.wikipedia.org/wiki/Tishrei).

13. The Maiden or Virgin (Virgo)

Maiden *Virgo* Aug 23–Sept 22		Northern Crown
		Herdsman *Bootes*
		Infant Prince *Coma*

Christ's Role: Immanuel, the promised Messiah
Summary: A *Virgin* will be the mother of an *Infant Prince*, who will become the King of Kings (*Crown*) and the Good Shepherd (*Herdsman*) who cares for and gives his life for his sheep.

"A *Virgin* shall be with child, and shall bring forth a son, and they shall call his name Immanuel" (Isa. 7:14; 2 Ne. 17:14; Matt. 1:23) which means "God with us." "For unto us a *child* is born, unto us a son is given; and the government shall be upon his shoulder; and his name shall be called, Wonderful Counselor, The Mighty God, The Everlasting Father, The *Prince* of Peace" (Isa. 9:6; 2 Ne. 19:6). "He will *reign* on David's throne and over his kingdom" (NIV Isa. 9:7).

An angel said, "The Lord Omnipotent ... shall go forth amongst men, working mighty miracles, such as healing the sick, raising the dead, causing the lame to walk, the blind to receive their sight, and the deaf to hear, and curing ... diseases. And he shall cast out devils, or the evil spirits which dwell in the hearts of the children of men. ... He shall suffer temptations, and pain of body, hunger, thirst, and fatigue, even more than man can suffer, except it be unto death; for behold, blood cometh from every pore, so great shall be his anguish for the wickedness and the abominations of his people. And he shall be called Jesus Christ, the Son of God, the Father of heaven and earth, the Creator of all things from the beginning; and his mother shall be called Mary. And lo, he cometh unto his own, ... [who] shall consider him a man, and ... shall scourge him, and shall crucify him. And he shall rise the third day from the dead ... to judge the world" (Mosiah 3:5–10).

John said "there appeared a great wonder [or sign] in heaven; a woman clothed with the sun, and the moon under her feet, and upon her head a crown of twelve stars. ... And to the woman were given two wings of a great eagle ... [to] fly into the wilderness" (Rev. 12:1, 14). Some believe this woman is Virgo, where the sun literally moves through her clothing when the moon is under her feet (Martin, 84–86). The Maiden (Virgo) is holding some wheat. The only bright star in Virgo is located in the wheat. Referring to his coming death, Jesus said, if "a grain of wheat ... dies, it bears much fruit" (RSV John 12:24).

14. The Balance or Scales (Libra)

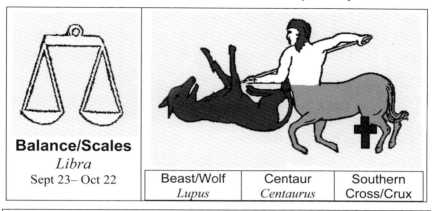

Balance/Scales *Libra* Sept 23– Oct 22	Beast/Wolf *Lupus*	Centaur *Centaurus*	Southern Cross/Crux

Christ's Role: Redeemer, Judge

Summary: Christ will be lifted up on the *Cross* to satisfy the demands of justice (*Balance*) and judge all mankind. The son of God, who is half mortal and half immortal (*Centaur*), will slay the wicked (*Wolves* and *Beasts*) who seek to kill the prophets and saints.

Anciently, "commercial transactions involved the use of weights and balances. ... God is often pictured in the Old Testament as a *judge* holding the *scales* ... measuring not only the motives but also the actions" (*DBI*, s.v. "Scales"; italics added).

Jesus said, "this is the gospel which I have given unto you—that I came into the world to do the will of my Father, because my Father sent me ... that I might be lifted up upon the *cross*; and ... as I have been lifted up by men even so should men be lifted up by the Father, to stand before me, to be *judged* of their works, whether they be good or whether they be evil ... And ... whoso repenteth and is baptized in my name shall be filled [with the Holy Ghost]; and if he endureth to the end, behold, him will I hold guiltless before my Father at that day when I shall stand to *judge* the world. And he that endureth not unto the end ... is also hewn down and cast into the fire, from whence they can no more return, because of the *justice* of the Father" (3 Ne. 27:13–21).

The "great and last sacrifice will be the Son of God ... to bring about the bowels of mercy, which overpowereth *justice*. ... And thus mercy can satisfy the demands of justice, and encircles them in the arms of safety ...; therefore only unto him that has faith unto repentance is brought about the great and eternal plan of redemption" (Alma 34:14–16).

15. The Scorpion (Scorpio)

Scorpion *Scorpius* Oct 23–Nov 21		Serpent *Serpens*
		Healer *Ophinchus*
		Altar *Ara*

Christ's Role: Master Physician or Healer, Atonement
Summary: Although Satan (*Scorpion*) may cause sickness or death by striking the heel with his tail, Christ (*Healer*) will crush sickness and death. Christ healed people "bitten by the poisonous serpents, if they would cast their eyes unto the *Serpent* which [Moses] did raise up" (2 Ne. 25:20). On *Altars*, we sacrifice or put off the natural man to get nearer to Christ.

God told the *Serpent* (Satan) that Christ (*Healer*), the seed or descendent of Eve, "will crush your head, and you will strike his heel" (NIV Gen. 3:15). Christ has power and gave to his disciples "power to tread on *Serpents* and *Scorpions*, and over all the power of the enemy" (Luke 10:19).

Poisonous *Serpents* symbolize death. Serpents also symbolize life, rebirth, and healing because they shed their skin and grow new skin (Skinner). When Israelites spoke against God, the LORD sent fiery serpents and many died. The LORD had Moses put a serpent of brass on a pole and all who looked at it lived (see Num 21:4–9; 2 Ne. 25:20; Alma 33:19–22; Hel. 8:14–15). Artists often depict the brass serpent on a cross (http://www.biblical-art.com/biblicalsubject2.asp?id_biblicalsubject=1266).

Moses and the Brass Serpent by Judith Mehr © Intellectual Reserve, Inc.

Today, the one snake "rod of Asclepius" and the two snake "caduceus" are used as symbols of medicine. The *rod of Asclepius* has been associated with medicine since the time of the Greeks. The *caduceus* was not associated with medicine before 1900. Of 242 organizations surveyed in 1992, 62% of professional associations used the *rod of Asclepius*, whereas 76% of commercial organizations and 63% of hospitals used the *caduceus* (Friedlander, 152–153; http://www.wikipedia.org, s.v. "Rod of Asclepius").

Rod of Asclepius   *Caduceus*

Healing was an emphasis of Christ's ministry. According to Leviticus, "atone means to cover or recover, repair a hole, cure a sickness, mend a rift, make good a torn or broken covering ... Atonement does not mean covering a sin so as to hide it from the sight of God; it means making good an outer layer which has rotted or been pierced" (Barker 2003, 45–6; quoting Mary Douglas; Barker 2004, 69).

Christ healed people who were separated from God and others so they could be temple worthy and reunited with God and the people. Sicknesses, deformities, injuries, and death separated people from the community or the temple. A Levite could not act as a priest if he had a "blemish," e.g., blind, lame, disfigured, deformed, crippled foot or hand, hunchback, dwarf, etc. (Lev. 21:16–23). Physical conditions that made a person unworthy (unclean) or unable to attend the temple or associate with others included leprosy and an issue of blood, palsy (paralysis), epilepsy, plague, and being possessed with a devil. The role of the high priest was to atone (cover, repair, restore, heal) that which separates people from the temple or the community and to bear or carry iniquities so the offender could be reintegrated into the community (Barker 2003, 48–49). Therefore, the great high priest, Christ, healed people of diseases and physical or spiritual conditions that made them unworthy or unable to participate in temple ordinances or to associate with the community. It is no wonder that prophecies of the savior's ministry focused on healing people as well as bearing their sins (Mosiah 3:5–8).

An *altar* is a place of sacrifice. *Sacrifice* comes from a Latin word, *sacrificium*, meaning to make sacred or holy. The Hebrew word, *korban*, signified "that which brings man near to God" (Rona 2001b, 18; quoting *Encyclopedia Judaica Jr.*). Korban "is from the same root as 'to come near, to approach... to become closely involved in a relationship with someone.'... The idea of a sacrifice or offering seems to indicate a gift or present. ... [However, *korban*] never carries a connotation of a present or gift, and is used exclusively by the Bible in the context of man's relationship with God. ... The goal of the Temple sacrifices is nothing less than the aim of dedicating human life to a higher sphere of awareness... closer to the Creator and the source of all life" (Richman, 13).

At temple altars and the sacrament table, people remember God, and make or renew covenants that bring them nearer to God (*Encyclopedia of Mormonism*, s.v. "Altar").

16. The Archer (Sagittarius)

Archer *Sagittarius* Nov 22–Dec 21	Kneeler *Hercules*
	Harp *Lyra*
	Dragon *Draco*

Christ's Role: LORD of Hosts (Armies)

Summary: Just as the *Archer* (half man, half horse) shoots the *Scorpion*, Christ (half God, and half man) will destroy Satan and his works. Like *Hercules*, Christ is the son of an immortal father and a mortal mother, and he later becomes immortal. In the fullness of times, Christ will subdue all enemies (*Dragon*) under his feet, and there shall be great rejoicing (*Harp*).

Jesus said, "when the earth is ripe ... all the proud and they that do wickedly shall be as stubble; and I will burn them up, saith the Lord of Hosts [armies], that wickedness shall not be upon the earth" (D&C 29:1–9).

The very wicked "are cast down to hell and suffer the wrath of Almighty God, until the fulness of times, when Christ shall have *subdued all enemies under his feet*" (D&C 76:106) "even to the *destroying of Satan* and his works at the end of the world" (D&C 19:2–3).

"There was war in heaven: Michael and his angels fought against the dragon ... and his angels. ... And the great *Dragon* was cast out, that old *serpent*, called the

Devil, and Satan; ... and his angels were cast out with him" (Rev. 12:7–9).

After being bound during the millennium for a thousand years, Satan will be loosed for a season. "And the devil shall gather together his armies ... and shall come up to battle against Michael and his armies ... and the devil and his armies shall be cast away into their own place, that they shall not have power over the saints any more at all" (D&C 88:110–114). Then, "the voice of a great multitude" will rejoice and praise Him at the "marriage supper of the Lamb" (Rev. 19:1–10).

"Rejoice in the LORD ... Praise the LORD with *harp*" (Ps. 33:1–2).

17. The Sea Goat (Capricorn)

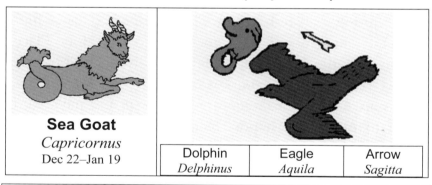

Sea Goat
Capricornus
Dec 22–Jan 19

Dolphin	Eagle	Arrow
Delphinus	*Aquila*	*Sagitta*

Christ's Role: Great and Last Sacrifice, Great High Priest
Summary: Christ was the great and last sacrifice (*Sea Goat*) who was pierced (*Arrow*) with nails and spear. He descended to the spirit world, resurrected (*Dolphin*), and ascended into heaven (*Eagle*).

"There should be a *great and last sacrifice* ... for the sins of the world ... and ... then shall the law of Moses be fulfilled. ... And ... that great and last sacrifice will be the Son of God, yea, infinite and eternal" (Alma 34:10–14).

On the Day of Atonement, the high priest "wore a golden seal on his forehead ... engraved only with the four letters of the sacred Name," YHWH which is translated as LORD in the KJV Bible. "The Mishnah describes how lots were drawn over the two *Goats*, and how the high priest pronounced the Name as the lot bearing the Name was drawn. This lot was inscribed in the same way as the seal which the high priest wore, and it was 'put on' the *Goat* before it was sacrificed. It was therefore the blood/life of the LORD which was brought out from the Holy of Holies to make the atonement. ... There was the high priest who 'was' the LORD, offering the blood/life of the LORD and taking this into the heaven, the holy of holies. The LORD was both the high priest and the offering. ... 'But, when Christ appeared as a high priest ... he entered once for all into the Holy Place, taking not the blood of goats and calves but his own blood' (Heb. 9:11–12)" (Barker 2004, 58, 64).

As an *Arrow* pierces its target, a spear and nails were used to pierce the hands, feet, and side of Christ (Ps. 22:16; John 19:34).

Going under the water represents death and coming out of the water (*Dolphin*) represents resurrection. "We are buried with him by baptism into death: that like as Christ was raised up from the dead by the glory of the Father, even so we also should walk in newness of life" (Rom. 6:4).

"They that wait upon the LORD shall renew their strength; they shall mount up with wings as *Eagles*; they shall run, and not be weary; and they shall walk, and not faint" (Isa. 40:31). The *Eagle*, king of the birds, is an "image of strength and deliverance" and "portrays the speed and power of both God's deliverance and God's destruction" or judgment (*DBI*, s.v. "eagle"). Birds also ascend from earth into the heavens as Christ ascended into heaven.

18. The Water Bearer (Aquarius)

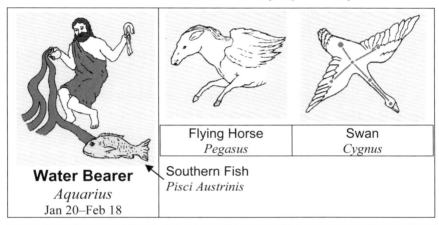

Water Bearer *Aquarius* Jan 20–Feb 18	Flying Horse *Pegasus*	Swan *Cygnus*
	Southern Fish *Pisci Austrinis*	

Christ's Role: Fountain of Living Water, King of Kings
Summary: Christ is the Fountain of Living Water (*Waterman*) who pours out his spirit and blessings on his church (*Southern Fish*). Like the ugly duckling that turned into a beautiful white *Swan*, Christ was despised and rejected by his peers but will return quickly (D&C 112:34) in power and glory as King of Kings (*Swan*) riding a white horse (*Flying Horse*) to victory over all enemies.

Christ is "the LORD, the *fountain of living waters*" (Jer. 17:13). His apostles became *fishers* of men to build up His church (*Fish*). On His disciples, Christ will pour out "living water," His spirit, blessings, and knowledge (John

4:10; D&C 19:38; 110:9–10; 121:33). Nephi said "the rod of iron ... was the word of God, which led to the *fountain of living waters*, or to the tree of life; which waters [and tree] are a representation of the love of God" (1 Ne. 11:25).

"Not all shepherds have a staff with a crook [like the *Water Bearer*]. It is only those who are descendents of the priestly and mighty line, having a strain of Egyptian blood. The crook designates that the shepherd has authority and dominion. ... Jesus as the good Shepherd is always depicted with a crook staff because 'All power is given unto Me in heaven and in Earth' (Matt. 28:18)" (Mountford 1914, 125, 128). The shepherd finds water and food for his sheep.

When John saw Christ coming in power at the second coming, the "King of Kings, and Lord of Lords" was riding "a *white horse*" as were the armies of heaven. "The beast, and the kings of the earth, and their armies gathered together to make war against him that sat on the horse, and against his army." The beast and the false prophet were "cast alive into a lake of fire" and the remnant was "slain with the sword" (Rev. 19:11–21).

The *Swan* is also known as the Northern Cross. The *Swan* is hanging upside down on the cross as did Peter when he was crucified. The resurrected Peter returned from heaven to restore priesthood.

19. The Fishes (Pisces)

Fishes	*Pisces*
Bands	Part of *Pisces*
Ram	*Aries*
Sea Monster	*Cetus*

Fishes
Pisces
Feb 19–Mar 20

Christ's Role: Deliverer, High Priest
Summary: Christ (*Ram*) breaks the *Bands* of death which bind his early and latter-day churches (*Fishes*) to the *Sea Monster*. Christ will subdue the *Sea Monster* under his feet.

As a male lamb becomes a *Ram*, the Lamb of God grew to manhood before He broke the bands of death. Christ "will take upon him death, that he may loose the *bands of death* which bind his people" (Alma 7:12). Christ "breaketh the *bands* of death, that the grave shall have no victory" (Alma 22:14). At His second coming, Christ "subdues all enemies under his feet" (D&C 58:22).

"O how great the goodness of our God, who prepareth a way for our escape from the grasp of this *awful monster* …, *death* and hell, which I call the *death of the body*, and also the death of the spirit. And because of the way of deliverance of our God, the Holy One of Israel, this death, … which is the temporal, shall deliver up its dead; which death is the grave" (2 Ne. 9:10–11).

God said to Abraham, "Take … thine only son Isaac … and get thee into the land of Moriah; and offer him there for a burnt offering upon one of the mountains which I will tell thee of" (Gen. 22:2). As Abraham was about to sacrifice his son, he saw "behind him a *ram* caught in a thicket by his horns: and Abraham went and took the ram, and offered him up for a burnt offering in the stead of his son" (Gen. 22:13). Mount Moriah is a major hill of Jerusalem where Solomon built the temple (2 Chr. 3:1). According to tradition, the Dome of the Rock is where Abraham offered Isaac. "A few hundred yards to the north on a higher point of that same hill system is ... Golgotha" where Christ was crucified (*OTSM*, 77). According to rabbinic tradition, "Isaac was in his early thirties when Abraham brought him to Mount Moriah. Jesus was sacrificed on the eve of his thirty-fourth birthday (the first day of Passover that year)" (Rona 2001b, 18).

20. The Ram (Aries)

Ram *Aries* Mar 21–Apr 19		King *Cepheus*
		Queen *Cassiopeia*
		Chained Princess *Andromeda*
		Hero *Perseus*

Christ's Role: Redeemer, Bridegroom

Summary: Through his atonement, Christ (*Ram*) becomes the *Hero* who frees his Church (*Chained Princess*) from the chains of hell. After "the marriage of the Lamb" to his Church, Christ becomes *King* and the glorified church becomes his *Queen*.

"The saints rejoiced in their redemption, and bowed the knee and acknowledged the Son of God as their Redeemer and Deliverer from death and the *chains of hell*" (D&C 138:23).

In Rev. 19:7, "the marriage of the Lamb, who is Christ (D&C 33:17–18) to his bride, who is the Church (D&C 109:73–74) as well as the New Jerusalem (D&C 21:2, 9–10), is a metaphor for the union between the Lord and his people, made possible through the atonement of Christ" (Parry and Parry, 251).

"For the atonement satisfieth the demands of his justice upon all those who have not the law given to them, that they are delivered from that *awful monster*, death and *hell*, and the devil …; and they are restored to that God who gave them breath, which is the Holy One of Israel. But wo unto him that has the law given, yea, that has all the commandments of God … and that transgresseth them, and that wasteth the days of his probation" (2 Ne. 9:26–27).

"We believe that through the Atonement of Christ, all mankind may be saved, by obedience to the laws and ordinances of the Gospel" (A of F 1:3).

"They that will harden their hearts, to them is given the lesser portion of the word until they know nothing concerning his mysteries; and then they are taken captive by the devil, and led by his will down to destruction. Now this is what is meant by the *chains of hell*" (Alma 12:11).

"O that ye would awake; awake from a deep sleep, yea, even from the sleep of hell, and shake off the awful *chains* by which ye are bound, which are the *chains* which bind the children of men, that they are carried away captive down to the eternal gulf of misery and woe" (2 Ne. 1:13).

21. The Bull or Wild Ox (Taurus)

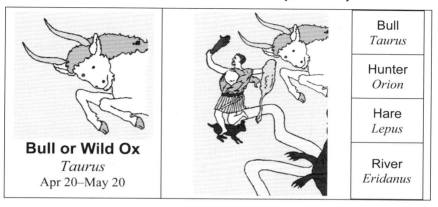

Bull	*Taurus*
Hunter	*Orion*
Hare	*Lepus*
River	*Eridanus*

Bull or Wild Ox
Taurus
Apr 20–May 20

> **Christ's Role:** Gathering of Israel, LORD of Hosts
> **Summary:** In the last days, Christ will use Ephraim (*Bull*) to gather Israel before he (*Hunter*) destroys the mother of harlots (*Hare*) who perverts religions and governments, and the wrath of God is poured out (*River*) on the wicked.

The white *Bull* or wild ox has a red star in its eye. Christ is described as having hair that is "white like the pure snow" and eyes "as a flame of fire" (D&C 110:3; Rev. 1:14). Oxen and bulls "suggest images of royalty, divinity, power, sacrifice, atonement, and Jehovah" (Gaskill, 257).

Moses compared Joseph to a bull with horns which represented his sons, Ephraim and Manasseh. "With them he shall push the people together to the ends of the earth" (Deut. 33:16–17). This appears to refer to the gathering of Israel in the last days (D&C 58:44–45) by the tribe of Ephraim. "In the last days their privilege and responsibility is to bear the priesthood, take the message of the restored gospel to the world, and raise an ensign to gather scattered Israel (Isa. 11:12–13; 2 Ne. 21:12–13)" (*GTS*, s.v. "Ephraim" and *BD*, s.v. "Ephraim"). The Book of Mormon is a record of the descendants of Lehi who was a descendant of Manasseh (Alma 10:3). When "the harvest is fully ripe ... and after the gathering of the wheat, behold ... the tares are bound in bundles, and the field remaineth to be burned" (D&C 86:7).

Rabbits represented immorality, adultery, fornication in antiquity and now, e.g., Playboy bunny (Gaskill, 246; italics added). When Christ "subdues all enemies under his feet" (D&C 58:22), this will include "Babylon the great, the mother of *harlots*" (Rev. 17:5). "The day cometh that the wrath of God is *poured out* upon the mother of *harlots*, which is the great and abominable church of all the earth, whose founder is the devil" (1 Ne. 14:15–17).

The LORD told Moses to have Aaron smite the *river* and it turned to blood and the fish died (Ex. 7:17–22). Likewise, John saw an angel pour out his vial upon the *rivers* and they became blood before the second coming (Rev. 16:4; 8:10–11).

22. The Twins (Gemini)

	Charioteer Shepherd *Auriga*
	Twins *Gemini*
Twins *Gemini* May 21–Jun 21	Little Dog *Canis Minor*
	Big Dog *Canis Major*

Christ's Role: Son of God
Summary: Like identical *Twins*, Christ is in the "express image" of his Father and to see one is to see the other. Like watchdogs, his ancient prophets and apostles (*Little Dog*) and those in the latter days (*Big Dog*) help protect the flock of the Good *Shepherd*.

Identical *twins* look alike. Christ is "the express image" (Heb. 1:3) or "exact representation" (NIV Heb. 1:3) of His Father's person as was Seth (D&C 138:40; Gen. 5:3). "He that hath seen me hath seen the Father" (John 14:9). "God created man … in the image of his own body" (Moses 6:8–9; Gen. 1:26). Jehovah showed himself to the brother of Jared and said, "all men were created in the beginning after mine own image. Behold, this body, which ye now behold, is the body of my spirit; and man have I created after the body of my spirit; and even as I appear unto thee to be in the spirit will I appear unto my people in the flesh" (Ether 3:15–16).

Orientals despise *dogs*. To call someone a dog is a great insult. However, some shepherds may use dogs. As a shepherd leads his flock, "dogs of [his] flock" (Job 30:1) "lag lazily behind the flocks ... [and bark] at any intruder ... [to warn of] danger" (Thomson, 593; Wight, 156, 269; *TDOT* 7:148–153). In other cultures, sheepdogs guide and protect sheep. The Egyptian dog-like god, Anubis, was guardian of the dead. He guided and protected souls on their journey to the underworld. As man's best friend, dogs guide the blind, save lives, and love and comfort their owners.

The *Shepherd* or *Charioteer* has a goat over his shoulder and some kids on his arm. A shepherd pastures his goats and sheep together but separates them in the sheepfold so that they get rest. Goats like to "butt and annoy the sheep, or dig their horns into their wool. ... He does not love the goats any less than the sheep" (Mountford, 1914, 138–139). Likewise, God will separate people into kingdoms according the law they are able to obey (D&C 88:21–25).

As Elijah and Elisha walked and talked, "there appeared a *chariot* of fire, and horses of fire, ... and Elijah went up by a whirlwind into heaven" (2 Kgs. 2:11). An archangel "conveyed [Enoch] in great glory on a fiery *chariot* ... up with the Šekinah to the heavenly heights" (3 Enoch 6:1; italics added). Enoch "saw the LORD" and Michael, the archangel, "anointed me with the delightful oil; ... its fragrance like myrrh; and its shining is like the sun. And ... I had become like one of the glorious ones" (2 Enoch 22:1, 8–10).

23. The Crab (Cancer)

| Crab
Cancer
Jun 22–Jul 22 | Ship
Argo | Little Bear
Ursa Minor | Big Bear
Ursa Major |

Christ's Role: Deliverer

Summary: Christ (*Crab*) liberated the captives in the spirit world. He calmed the sea to preserve his disciples and Lehi's family who were traveling in their *Ships* during storms. He guides and protects his sheep like a mother bear (*Big Bear*) guides and protects her cub (*Little Bear*).

Crabs shed their shells 1 to 12 times a year. While the new shell hardens, crabs may bury themselves for about *three days* to hide from predators. A crab can descend into the sea, grab things with its claws, and return to dry land. Likewise, Christ was buried, descended into the spirit world (GR: *hades*), proclaimed liberty to the captives who would repent (D&C 138; Isa. 61:1; Luke 4:18), and after three days returned with a resurrected body. Christ said, "My sheep ... follow me ... and they shall never perish, neither shall any man pluck them out of my hand" (John 10:27–28).

Ships allow people to travel on and fish in the sea. The sea, known as the Deep or the Abyss, symbolizes the forces of chaos, evil and destruction (*DBI*, 171). It also denotes the underworld of the dead (Rom. 10:7) and demons (Gaskill, 398 n. 76, 400 n. 42). Hurricanes and tidal waves threaten the lives of people on land or in ships. Sea monsters also threaten the lives of people. God controls the sea and the sea monsters. The ark saved Noah from the floods that destroyed the wicked (Gen. 7). When Jonah got on the ship, the LORD sent a storm and the great fish that swallowed Jonah (Jonah 1). "The LORD caused the sea to go back," saving the Israelites, and then to return, drowning the Egyptians (Ex. 14:21–30). Christ calmed the stormy sea to save his disciples (Mark 4:37–41). He walked on the sea (Matt. 14:22–32). After commanding Nephi to build a ship, God sent a storm to humble Laman and Lemuel, calmed the sea, and guided Lehi's family to the promised land (1 Ne. 17–18).

A mother *Bear* guides and protects her cubs or whelps (Hosea 13:8; Prov. 17:12). In the Millennium, "the cow and the bear shall feed; their young ones shall lie down together" (2 Ne. 21:7; 30:13). *Little Bear* appears to follow *Big Bear* during the night. Ancient seamen used the stars as guides because their magnetic compasses were unreliable. People use the big dipper (*Big Bear*) and the little dipper (*Little Bear*) to find the North Star. At night, sailors could use the North Star to determine directions, the time, and their latitude.

24. The Lion (Leo)

Lion
Leo
Jul 23–Aug 22

Raven	Cup	Sea Serpent
Corvus	*Crater*	*Hydra*

Christ's Role: King

Summary: When the *Cup* of his wrath is full, Christ will pour out his wrath on the mother of harlots who holds a *Cup* full of abominations. The fowls of the air (*Raven*) shall devour the wicked and Satan (*Sea Serpent*) shall be bound for a thousand years. Christ will dwell on earth as King (*Lion*) and lawgiver after he has subdued all enemies (*Sea Serpent*) under his feet.

The *Lion*, king of the beasts, is associated with Judah (Gen. 49:9), the tribe of Judah, and the house of David (*Encyclopedia Judaica*, s.v. "Lion"). The bright star at the heart of the Lion is Regulus which means "little king" or prince. Christ, the Lion of Judah (Rev. 5:5), will receive the throne of his ancestor, King David (Luke 1:30–33). He will subdue all enemies *under his feet* (D&C 49:6; 76:104–108) and will "dwell in righteousness with men on earth a thousand years" (D&C 29:11) as "their king (*Lion*) and their lawgiver" (D&C 45:55–59).

When the *Cup* of his *wrath* and *indignation* is full, Christ will *pour out* his wrath on "the mother of harlots, … the great and abominable church ... [of] the devil" because she has "a golden *Cup* in her hand full of abominations and filthiness of her fornication" (Rev. 17:4; 1 Ne. 14:17; D&C 43:26–33). "The fowls of the air (*Raven*) shall devour them up. And the great and abominable church, which is the whore of all the earth, shall be cast down by devouring fire" (D&C 29:20–21).

An angel will lay "hold on the *dragon*, that old *Serpent*, which is the Devil, and Satan, and [bind] him a thousand years" (Rev. 20:1–2). "In that day the LORD with his sore and great and strong sword shall punish leviathan the piercing *Serpent*, even leviathan that crooked *Serpent*; and he shall slay the *dragon* that *is* in the sea" (Isa. 27:1).

Conclusion

If these twenty-four nature ornaments were used from December 1st to the 24th, the *Crab* ornament that relates to the spirit world would be put on the tree on December 23rd, the birthday of Joseph Smith, who restored temple work for the dead. The *Lion* ornament that represents the second coming would be put on the tree on Christmas Eve when we celebrate his first coming.

Nature ornaments could be pictures or drawings mounted on a bottle lid or thick paper. They could also be objects like a small rock. They could be placed on an Advent tree or displayed on an Advent calendar. (See http://www.summitviewpublishing.com for links to a colored version of the pictures used in the text.)

If families discussed these or other scriptural symbols for the twenty-four days before each Christmas, it would help them remember Christ always because we see, hear, and read about these symbols throughout the year.

4

HAVE A "MARY" CHRISTMAS

Before the first Christmas, Mary pondered the words of the angel Gabriel and the prophecies about her firstborn son. When she was troubled, Gabriel said "Fear not." Mary asked "How shall this be, seeing I know not a man?" The angel said "with God nothing shall be impossible" and reminded her that her barren cousin Elisabeth had conceived a son in her old age (Luke 1:26–38). Faith replaced fear and doubt. Over the next year, Mary's experience confirmed her faith. She gave birth to the *king of kings* in a cave and laid him in a manger. Ironically, from Bethlehem she could see Herodium, one of King Herod's palaces, only three miles away. After Jesus' birth, she focused her attention on him and continued to ponder the prophecies about her son.

She Shall Bring Forth A Son © Liz Lemon Swindle

Like Mary, we can remember, ponder and discuss the prophecies and accounts of Christ's birth, life, mission, teachings, death, and resurrection. We can also seek to know and do God's will with faith, knowing that "with God nothing shall be impossible" (Luke 1:37).

Another Mary sat at the feet of Jesus while her sister "Martha was *cumbered* about much serving." Martha said, "Lord, dost thou not care that my sister hath left me to serve alone? bid her therefore that she help me. And Jesus ... said unto her, Martha, Martha, thou art *careful* and *troubled* about many things: But one thing is *needful*: and Mary hath chosen that good part, which shall not be taken away from her" (Luke 10:38–42).

Mary and Martha by Del Parson © by Intellectual Reserve, Inc.

In her book *Can Martha Have a Mary Christmas*, Brenda Poinsett refers to Christmas as "the most Martha time of the year." "For most women, the mention of Christmas creates visions of meals to cook, gifts to buy, cards to mail, parties to organize, and tons of events to attend. And somewhere in the mix, it's easy to feel empty and lose sight of Jesus. It's a scene the biblical Martha would easily recognize. As she bustled around her house caring for her hungry guests, her sister Mary sat peacefully at the feet of Jesus. We all want to be like Mary, resting at the feet of Christ. But during the busiest season of the year, the 'Martha' role seems to be inevitable for women. How can we push aside the busyness of the season and get a true glimpse of Christ at Christmas?" (Poinsett, 11, back cover).

Remembering Christ at Christmas suggests possible ways to have a more "Mary" Christmas by viewing or doing some things a little differently. Chapter 1 suggests ways of looking at common Christmas traditions as links to remind us of Christ. The different nativity stories in chapter 2 help us ponder other possibilities as we see a nativity play or read the nativity story with our families on Christmas Eve. Chapter 3 presents ways of using the common tradition of advent calendars or trees differently. There are many other ways to remember Christ at Christmas. Our family traditions include baking, caroling, donating to projects like Sub-for-Santa, and visiting rest homes. We also attend Christmas parties which provide us with the opportunity to enjoy, love, and serve others.

The Christmas season always offers more worthwhile possibilities than anyone can ever do. It is like going to an all-you-can-eat restaurant where there are more good things to eat than one can possibly enjoy. If we eat too little, we will be hungry. If we eat only desserts, our bodies will not receive adequate nourishment. If we eat too much, pleasure turns into misery. While some people leave the restaurant filled and content, others may feel upset that they ate too much or too little. "In choosing how we spend time as a family, we should be careful not to exhaust our available time on things that are merely good and leave little time for that which is better or best. ... Some uses of individual and family time are better, and others are best. We have to *forego some good things* in order to choose others that are *better* or *best* because they develop faith in the Lord Jesus Christ and strengthen our families" (Oaks; italics added). As we ponder and discuss the Christmas "menu" and what Jesus would have us do, spiritual promptings will help us *feel* what is good, better, and best for us as individuals or as a family.

We can learn another lesson from Martha. It is easy to get upset when others do what they prefer instead of what we think they should do. We might try to command or compel them to do our will. Like Martha we may even ask someone else to apply a little extra pressure on them. If they still choose otherwise, we often become "travel agents for guilt trips." As a result, the spirit of contention and frustration replaces the spirit of love. My wife shares an example of this in the following anecdote about some of her Christmas expectations.

> As a child, my family enjoyed the tradition of Christmas caroling. Everyone in our home loved to sing and we usually went caroling on several different nights, taking music and an over-flowing plate of homemade goodies to the elderly, the shut-ins, and the less active members of our ward. We were warmly welcomed into their homes and often accepted the invitation to sit down and visit.
>
> When my own children were old enough to sing, I eagerly implemented this tradition. At first they all seemed to share my

delight in preparing the goodies and singing our favorite Christmas songs as we delivered the treats to our neighbors. But as our sons approached their teen years they began to resist, especially when we stopped to visit. I was frustrated that they didn't savor this experience like I did because I felt it was the perfect way to teach them the true meaning of Christmas. As each Christmas season rolled around I tried various methods of rewarding them or otherwise applying pressure in an effort to get them to comply with my wishes. Although I could persuade them to go to a few homes if we didn't stay too long, none of them wanted to do as much caroling and visiting as I did.

Finally I opened my mind to other possibilities. We chose a night for family caroling and let our children select the homes we would go to. Everyone in the family was invited and encouraged to participate, but no one was compelled. Then, to satisfy my desire for more caroling and visiting, I organized caroling nights with other sisters in the ward who love to sing as much as I do. Although we still invite our adult children and their families to go Christmas caroling with us when they are available, I now have another favorite Christmas tradition of caroling with my friends.

When we recognized that the "Martha" approach was not working, we began inviting and enticing (Moro. 7:13) our children to go caroling with us and then allowed them to choose. We were pleasantly surprised at how often they chose to join us and by their positive comments afterwards. This change helped all of us have a *merry* "Mary" Christmas.

Of course the best way to always remember Christ at Christmas and throughout the year is to become more like Him by loving God and neighbor as He loves us. "For how knoweth a man the master whom he has not served, and who is a stranger unto him, and is far from the thoughts and intents of his heart?" (Mosiah 5:13).

Have a merry "Mary" Christmas!

APPENDIX: MADAME LYDIA MOUNTFORD
(1848–1917)

Madame Mountford was born in Jerusalem in 1848. Her parents were of "noble Russian birth" and had non-sectarian Christian beliefs. Her father entertained Apostle Orson Hyde in Jerusalem in the early 1840s. He wanted to know more about Joseph Smith and the "golden Bible." In Feb. 1897, Lydia came to Salt Lake City "and gave a lecture ... which was heard by Dr. James E. Talmage, who was president of the Latter-day Saints University at the time. He was so impressed with the wonder and beauty of her work that arrangements were made for her to deliver her series of lectures in the Tabernacle. ... The Madame remained three weeks in Salt Lake, giving her lectures in the Tabernacle, ... sometimes between nine and ten thousand people forming the audience. ... Her lectures took up phases of the Savior's life, illustrating his parables and his life and death, by a group of people costumed in real Arabian and Jewish robes and turbans. ... The Madame came to Provo, and delivered her lectures under the auspices of the Brigham Young University, to packed houses in the Provo tabernacle. Benjamin Cluff, who was then president of the University, arranged a series of lectures throughout the state. ... Crowds followed her everywhere. ... Madame Mountford was baptized into our Church, when she was here, in 1897, but kept on with her regular lecture work, and finally died ... in Florida, while delivering a series of lectures" in 1917 (*The Relief Society Magazine*, vol. 8.2, Feb. 1921, 71–76).

In the Holy Land, at least before 1930, the peasant shepherds lived in villages and kept their ancient customs, costumes, and traditions. Although most peasants were Muslims, some villages were entirely Christian (Whiting, 1926, 729; 1914, 249, 270).

In the introduction to her lectures, Madam Mountford said, "I was born in the city of Jerusalem, brought up in the city of Jerusalem, and I know the whole country of Palestine. ... Probably you are not familiar with the traditional Christ, such as we have Him, *handed down by tradition* from father to son, from chieftain to tribe, from elders to community, from mother to daughter—this Christ that is spoken of at the fireside, around the campfire, on the other side of Jordan. You know Paul says to us, 'Stand steadfast by the traditions you have been taught, either by word or by our epistle' (2 Thes. 2:15). When we teach by an epistle, the man gives his epistle, and it is copied by two or three hundred scribes ... and each one keeps a copy of the epistle, and that is called *teaching by epistle*. And there is what is called *teaching by word*. And teaching by word can never be written. It is handed down in song and story; and you listen to these stories of the elders and chieftains from the beginning of creation to the present day, and then they take those and elaborate on them in song and in story. ... The Gospels are ... more or less fragmentary. It was the business of the recorder simply to record salient facts. The other information was generally known, and they were recording facts, in order to show that Jesus was the Son of God. And so tonight we shall study the history of Christ from these traditions as we have them in His homeland, and I will recite them to you as they are given to us" (Mountford, 1911, 7–9; italics added).

Madam Mountford has written two books based on her lectures: *Jesus Christ in His Homeland* and *The King of the Shepherds and His Psalm*.

BIBLIOGRAPHY

The bibliography for "Illustrations" comes after "Books and Articles."

See http://www.SummitViewPublishing.com for links to online articles and illustrations.

A. Books and Articles

ABRAMS III, Cooper P, "Where was the Birth Place of the Lord Jesus?" http://www.bible-truth.org/BirthPlaceofJesus.html.

ADAMSON, Diane G., *I Believe In Santa Claus*, (1998).

BARKER, Margaret. 2003. *The Great High Priest*. London: T & T Clark.

———. 2004. *Temple Theology*. London: Society for Promoting Christian Knowledge.

BARNEY, Kevin. 2006. "Christmas in Israel." http://www.bycommonconsent.com/2006/11/christmas-in-israel.

BENNETT, Robert R. 2000. "Jesus' Birthplace and the Phrase 'Land of Jerusalem'." http://MaxwellInstitute.byu.edu.

BENSON, Ezra Taft. 1993. "First Presidency Message: Keeping Christ in Christmas." *Ensign*, Dec. 1993, 2–5.

Bible Dictionary. 1981. Salt Lake City: The Church of Jesus Christ of Latter-day Saints.

BLACK, Susan Easton. 2001. *Son of Man: Jesus Christ, The Early Years*. Shelton, Conn.: Greenwich Workshop Press.

Boy Scout Handbook. 1998. 11th ed. Irving, TX: Boy Scouts of America.
BRODERICK, Carlfred. 1996. *My Parents Married on a Dare.* Salt Lake City: Deseret Book.
BROOKS, Garth. 1990. "Unanswered Prayers." Song lyrics.
BROWN, S. Kent. 2005. "Zacharias and Elisabeth, Joseph and Mary." *LTJC,* I:91–120.
BUCK, Deanna Draper. 2006. *My First Story of the First Christmas.* Salt lake City: Deseret Book. [No page numbers.]
EDERSHEIM, Alfred. 1883. *The Life and Times of Jesus the Messiah.* New York: Longmans, Green, & Co. Photolithoprinted by Eerdmans (1981).
Encyclopedia Judaica. 1972. Edited by Geoffrey Wigoder. 16 vols. Jerusalem: Keter.
Encyclopedia of Mormonism. 1992. Edited by Daniel H. Ludlow. 5 vols. New York: Macmillan. [See also http://www.lib.byu.edu/Macmillan.]
FARRAR, Frederic W. 1874. *The Life of Christ.* New York: E.P. Dutton.
FRIEDLANDER, Walter J. 1992. *The Golden Wand of Medicine: A History of the Caduceus Symbol in Medicine.* New York: Greenwood Press.
GASKILL, Alonzo L. 2003. *The Lost Language of Symbolism.* Salt Lake City: Deseret Book.
GEIKIE, Cunningham. 1891. *The Life and Words of Christ.* New York: Columbia.
GOWER, Ralph. 1987. *The New Manners and Customs of Bible Times.* Chicago: Moody Press.
GRIGGS, C. Wilfred. 1988. "The Tree of Life in Ancient Cultures." *Ensign,* June 1988, 26–31.

———. 2003, *"Tree of life in Ancient Cultures." Book of Mormon Reference Companion.* Edited by Dennis L. Largey. Salt Lake City: Deseret Book.

Guide to the Scriptures. 2001. In *The Scriptures: CD-ROM Edition 1.1.* Salt Lake City: The Church of Jesus Christ of Latter-day Saints.

HEGSTED, Derek J. Forthcoming. *On My Way to Galilee.* http://www.hegsted.com

HINCKLEY, Gordon B. 1983. "What Shall I Do Then with Jesus Which Is Called Christ?" *Ensign,* Dec. 1983, 2–5.

———. 1997. "A Season for Gratitude," *Ensign,* Dec. 1997, 2.

HOLZAPFEL, Richard Neitzel, Eric D. HUNTSMAN, and Thomas A. WAYMENT. 2006. *Jesus Christ and the World of the New Testament.* Salt Lake City: Deseret Book.

HOLZAPFEL, Richard Neitzel and Thomas A. WAYMENT. 2003–2006. *The Life and Teachings of Jesus Christ.* 3 vols. Salt Lake City: Deseret Book.

HULBERT, Terry C. "Jesus' Birth." http://www.ancientsandals.com/articles/01_jesus_birth.htm.

HUNTER, Howard W. 1972. "The Real Christmas." *BYU Speeches,* Dec. 5, 1972.

HUMPHREYS, C.J., and W.G. WADDINGTON, 1989. "Astronomy and the Date of the Crucifixion." *Chronos, Kairos, Christos.* Edited by J. Vardaman and E.M. Yamauchi. Winona Lake: Eisenbrauns. 165–181.

Hymns of The Church of Jesus Christ of Latter-day Saints. Salt Lake City: The Church of Jesus Christ of Latter-day Saints.

International Standard Bible Encyclopedia. 1939. Grand Rapids, Mich.: Wm. B. Eerdmans. [See "Study Dictionary" at http://net.bible.org.]

KATIE, Byron. 2003. *Loving What Is*. New York: Three Rivers Press.

KEIL, C. F. and F. DELITZSCH. 1983–1984. *Commentary on the Old Testament*. Grand Rapids, Mich.: Eerdmans.

KIMBALL, Spencer W. 1980. "Remarks and Dedication of the Fayette, New York, Buildings." *Ensign*, May 1980, 54, 59; General Conference.

LEE, Harold B. 1973. "Strengthen the Stakes of Zion." *Ensign*, July 1973, 2–6; General Conference.

LEHRMAN, S. M., trans. 1983. *Midrash Rabbah: Exodus*. London: Soncino Press.

MARTIN, Ernest L. 1998. *The Star That Astonished the World*, 2d ed. Portland, OR: Academy for Scriptural Knowledge.

MAXWELL, Neal A. 2004. "Remember How Merciful the Lord Hath Been." *Ensign*, May 2004, 44–46.

MCCONKIE, Bruce R. 1979. *The Mortal Messiah*. 4 vols. Salt Lake City: Deseret Book.

MCCONKIE, Joseph Fielding and Donald W. PARRY. 1990. *A Guide to Scriptural Symbols*. Salt Lake City: Bookcraft.

MILLER, Jeanette W. 1993. "The Tree of Life, A Personification of Christ." *FARMS Journal of Book of Mormon Studies*, Vol. 2, #1 (Spring, 1993), 93–106. http://MaxwellInstitute.byu.edu.

MONSON, Thomas S. 2006. "First Presidency Message: Treasured Gifts." *Ensign*, December 2006, 5–10.

MOUNTFORD, Lydia M. Von Finkelstein. 1911: *Jesus Christ in His Homeland*. Cincinnati, OH: Press of Jennings and Graham.

———. 1914. *The King of the Shepherds and His Psalm*. Cincinnati, OH: Abingdon Press.

New Testament Stories. 1980, 2005. Salt Lake City: The Church of Jesus Christ of Latter-day Saints.

NELSON, Russell M. 2002. "Christ the Savior Is Born." *BYU Devotional*, 10 Dec. 2002, 1–5. http://speeches.byu.edu.

NIBLEY, Hugh. 1993. *Teachings of the Book of Mormon: Semester 1*. Provo, UT: FARMS.

———. 2005, *The Message of the Joseph Smith Papyri: An Egyptian Endowment*. 2d ed. Salt Lake City: Deseret Book

NIELSEN, Donna B. 1999. *Beloved Bridegroom*. Salt Lake City: Onyx Press.

———. 2007. *Holy Child Jesus*. Salt Lake City: Onyx Press. [Talk on audio CD.]

OAKS, Dallin H. 2007. "Good, Better, Best" *Ensign*, Nov. 2007, 104–8.

OGDEN, D. Kelly and Andrew C. SKINNER. 2006. *Verse by Verse: The Four Gospels*. Salt Lake City: Deseret Book.

Old Testament Student Manuel Genesis–2 Samuel. 1980–1981. Prepared by the Church Educational System. Salt Lake City: The Church of Jesus Christ of Latter-day Saints.

PARRY, Donald W. 1994. "Garden of Eden: Prototype Sanctuary." *Temples of the Ancient World*. Edited by Donald W. Parry. Salt Lake City: Deseret Book, 133–137.

PARRY, Jay A. and Donald W. PARRY. 1998. *Understanding the Book of Revelation*. Salt Lake City: Deseret Book.

PFANN, Stephen and Claire. 1993. "New Light on an Old, Old Story: Jesus' Birth at Bethlehem." http://www.uhl.ac/christmasStory.html.

POINSETT, Brenda. 2005. *Can Martha Have a Mary Christmas?* Birmingham: New Hope Publishers.

PRATT, John P. [All articles can be found at http://www.JohnPratt.com.]

———. 1990. "Yet another Eclipse for Herod." *The Planetarian*, vol. 19, no.4, Dec. 1990, 8–14.

———. 1994. "Passover: Was it Symbolic of His Coming?" *Ensign*, Jan. 1994, 38–45.

———. 2001. "The Constellations Testify of Christ." *Meridian Magazine*, Oct. 9, 2001.

———. 2004. "Review of Gospel in the Stars." 10 July 2004.

———. 2005. "The Constellations Tell of Christ." *Meridian Magazine*, June 2005.

RICHMAN, Chaim. 1997. *The Holy Temple of Jerusalem*. Jerusalem: The Temple Institute & Carta.

ROMNEY, President Marion G. 1972. "What Would Jesus Do?" *New Era*, Sept. 1972, 4–6.

———. 1973. "Magnifying One's Calling in the Priesthood." *Ensign*, July 1973, 89–91.

RONA, Daniel. http://www.israelrevealed.com.

———. 2001a, *Israel Revealed*. Salt Lake City: Ensign Foundation.

———. 2001b, *Old Testament Supplement Study Materials*. Salt Lake City: Ensign Foundation.

SANDERS, E. P. 1992. *Judaism: Practice and Belief 63 BCE – 66 CE*. London: Trinity Press International.

SATTERFIELD, Bruce. N.d. "Seeing *Christ* in Today's *Christ*mas." http://emp.byui.edu/SatterfieldB/Papers.

SAXE, John Godfrey. "Blind Men and the Elephant." (Do internet search.)

SHELLEY, Monte F. *When Was Jesus Born, Baptized, and Buried? — A Review of LDS and Non-LDS Educated Guesses.* [See http://www.summitviewpublishing.com for more information.]

SKINNER, Andrew. 2001. "Serpent Symbols and Salvation in the Ancient Near East and the Book of Mormon." *Journal of Book of Mormon Studies* 10:2:42–55 (2001). http://MaxwellInstitute.byu.edu.

SPECKMAN, Stephen. 2005. "Teacher's cause is anti-Claus," *Deseret Morning News* (Dec. 1, 2005).

TVERBERG, Lois. 2004a. "Of Standing Stones and Christmas Trees." http://www.egrc.net. Search for "Christmas."

———. 2004b. "Acts of Loving Kindness at Christmas," http://www.egrc.net. Search for "Christmas."

THOMSON, William M. *The Land and the Book.* (1954: Baker Book House; 1880–86: Harper & brothers).

TVEDTNES, John A. 1998. "What Do We Know about the Wise Men?" *FARMS Insights*, 18:12. See also http://MaxwellInstitute.byu.edu.

VERCELLONE, Carlo. *Biblionum Sacrorum Graecus* **Codex Vaticanus** (facsimile), (1868–1881: Romae: Typis et impensis S. Congregationis de propaganda fide).

WALKER, Williston. 1970. *History of the Christian Church*, 3d ed. New York: Scribner.

WELCH, John W. 2007. "The Good Samaritan: Forgotten Symbols." *Ensign*, Feb 2007, 40–47.

WHITING, John D. 1914. "Village Life in the Holy Land." *National Geographic*, 25:3 (Mar. 1914), 249–314.

———. 1926. "Among the Bethlehem Shepherds." *National Geographic*, 50:6 (Dec. 1926), 729–753.

———. 1929. "Bethlehem and the Christmas Story." *National Geographic*, 56:6 (Dec. 1929), 698–735.

———. 1937. "Bedouin Life in Bible Lands" *National Geographic*, 71:1 (Jan. 1937), 58–83.

WIGHT, Fred H. 1953. *Manners and Customs of Bible Lands*. Chicago: Moody Press.

WITHROW, W. H. 1877. *The Catacombs of Rome*. London: Hodder & Stoughton.

B. Illustrations

American Colony Photographers, Jerusalem. [Later known as *Matson Photo Service*. Photographs in the G. Eric and Edith Matson Photograph Collection are in the public domain. http://www.loc.gov/rr/print/res/258_mats.html.]

———. "House built over a cave used as a stable." (Whiting, 1914, 310)

———. "Mother holding baby in swaddling clothes." (Whiting, 1929, 711)

AVI, Deror. "Herod's Temple." http://en.wikipedia.org/wiki/Image:P8170082.jpg. Model in the Jerusalem Museum.

BEYER, Dirk. "Campfire." http://commons.wikimedia.org/wiki/Image:Campfire_4213.jpg. [This work is licensed under the Creative Commons Attribution-Share Alike License. To view a copy of this license, visit http://creativecommons.org/licenses/by-sa/2.5/ or send a letter to Creative Commons, 559 Nathan Abbott Way, Stanford, California 94305, USA.]

BOLEN, Todd. "Gezer." BiblePlaces.com. http://www.bibleplaces.com/gezer.htm.

BRICKEY, Joseph. "Journey to Bethlehem." http://olivewoodbooks.com. Used by permission.

"Caduceus." http://commons.wikimedia.org/wiki/Image:Caduceus.svg. Public domain. [Two snakes on a cross.]
"Chi-Rho." http://commons.wikimedia.org/wiki/Image:Simple_Labarum.gif. Public domain.
"Christmas Tree." http://commons.wikimedia.org/wiki/Image:Christmas_tree_in_Texas.jpg. Public domain.
"Christus Statue, Temple Square." http://commons.wikimedia.org/wiki/Image:Christus_statue_temple_square_salt_lake_city.jpg. Public domain.
Clipart
———. "Candy Cane."
———. "Christmas Stocking."
———. "Mistletoe."
———. "Santa at chimney."
———. "Santa's Sleigh and Reindeer."
DA SIENA, Barna. Died 1351(?). "The Birth of Jesus." Fresco. Detail of The Nativity. Collegiata. San Gimignano. In *The Life of Christ*, © In the English Edition, Wm. Collins Sons & Co. Ltd., 1959.
DEWEY, Simon. http://www.altusfineart.com.
———. "For God So Loved the World." Used by permission.
———. "We Three Kings." Used by permission.
DONATUS, Darko Tepert. "Stone Manger at Meggido." http://commons.wikimedia.org/wiki/Image:Meggido_Manger.jpg. [This work is licensed under the Creative Commons Attribution-Share Alike License. To view a copy of this license, visit http://creativecommons.org/licenses/by-sa/2.5 or send a letter to Creative Commons, 559 Nathan Abbott Way, Stanford, California 94305, USA.]

GHOLIZADEH, Babak. "Caravansary." http://commons.wikimedia.org/wiki/Image:Caravansarai_Karaj.jpg. [This work is licensed under the Creative Commons Attribution-Share Alike License. To view a copy of this license, visit http://creativecommons.org/licenses/by-sa/2.5/ or send a letter to Creative Commons, 559 Nathan Abbott Way, Stanford, California 94305, USA.]

HEGSTED, Derek J. http://www.hegsted.com.

———. "Angel at Gethsemane." Used by permission.

———. "Gethsemane Grove." Used by permission.

———. "Golgotha." Used by permission.

———. "Journey's End." Used by permission.

———. "Tree of Life." Used by permission.

HUNT, Jason. "Elephant illustration." http://www.naturalchild.com/jason/blind_men_elephant.html. Used by permission.

ICHTHYS or Fish Symbol. http://commons.wikimedia.org/wiki/Image:Ichthus.svg. Public domain.

Intellectual Reserve, Inc. http://www.lds.org. All images used by permission.

———. "Announcement of Christ's Birth to the Shepherds" by Del Parson. http://www.lds.org/hf/art/0,16812,4218-1-2,00.html.

———. "Moses and the Brass Serpent" by Judith Mehr. http://www.lds.org/hf/art/0,16812,4218-1-1,00.html.

———. "The Good Samaritan" by Walter Rane. http://www.lds.org/hf/art/0,16812,4218-1-2,00.html.

———. "Lehi's Dream" by Jerry Thompson. *Book of Mormon Stories.* 1997: The Church of Jesus Christ of Latter-day Saints. 20.

———. "Jesus Praying in Gethsemane" by Harry Anderson. http://www.lds.org/hf/art/0,16812,4218-1-2,00.html.

———. "Mary and Martha" by Del Parson. http://swww.lds.org/hf/art/0,16812,4218-1-2,00.html.
———. "Swaddling Bands." http://www.lds.org/pa/display/0,17884,7244-1,00.html. [Still from "Savior of the World."]
———. "Wise Men Bearing Gifts" by Paul Mann. *New Testament Stories*. 1995–2005: The Church of Jesus Christ of Latter-day Saints. 18.
———. "Wise Men Follow the Star" by Paul Mann. *New Testament Stories*. 1995–2005: The Church of Jesus Christ of Latter-day Saints. 18.
Jain World. "Elephant and the Blind Men." http://www.jainworld.com. Used by permission. Search for "elephant."
KATSURA, Hidetomo. "3-D Teapot." http://www.katsurashareware.com. Used by permission.
"Lambs." http://commons.wikimedia.org/wiki/Image:Lamb.jpg. Public domain.
"Latin Cross." http://commons.wikimedia.org/wiki/Image:Christian_cross.svg. Public domain.
MCINTOSH, Peter. "Lightning Storm." http://www.mcintoshmountains.com. Used by permission.
"Menorah." http://commons.wikimedia.org/wiki/Image:Menorah.svg. Public domain.
"Moon, Venus and Stars." http://coolcosmos.ipac.caltech.edu/cosmic_kids/AskKids/venus_sky.shtml. [May be used without prior permission. See http://www.spitzer.caltech.edu/Media/mediaimages/copyright.shtml.]
Northumberland. http://ngfl.northumberland.gov.uk.
———. "No Room at the Inn." Used by permission. Search for "clipart inn."

OGDEN, D. Kelly. "Bethlehem and Shepherds' Fields." Used by permission.
———. "Church of the Nativity." Used by permission. http://relarchive.byu.edu. Search for title "nativity."
———. "Fishermen on Sea of Galilee." Used by permission. http://relarchive.byu.edu. Search for "fishermen."
———. "Grotto of the Nativity." Used by permission. http://relarchive.byu.edu. Search for "nativity."
———. "Judean Wilderness." Used by permission. http://relarchive.byu.edu. Search for "wilderness."
———. "Olive Tree in Gethsemane." Used by permission. http://relarchive.byu.edu. Search for "olive."
———. "Two likely routes." Used by permission.
PARSON, Del. http://www.delparson.com.
———. "American Prophet." Used by permission.
———. "Birth of Jesus." Used by permission.
———. "Gentle Christ." Used by permission.
———. "The Good Shepherd." Used by permission.
PRATT, John. "49 Constellations." http://www.johnpratt.com/items/docs/lds/meridian/2006/49constellations.html. [All images of constellations used by permission.]
"Rod of Asclepius." http://commons.wikimedia.org/wiki/Image:Asclepius_staff.svg. Public domain. [One snake on a cross.]
"Rubin's Goblet-Profile." http://en.wikipedia.org/wiki/Image:Rubin2.jpg. Public domain.
"Santa Claus." http://commons.wikimedia.org/wiki/Image:Santa_usairforce.jpg. Public domain. [Picture from the Clear Air Force Station Homepage http://www.clear.af.mil.]

"Sunset in Israel." http://commons.wikimedia.org/wiki/Image:Sunsetinisrael.jpg. Public domain.

SHELLEY, Monte F.

———. "Advent Calendar."

———. "Advent tree: Children watching as a decoration is added."

———. "Animal Montage." Made from public domain images at http://commons.wikimedia.org and at http://en.wikipedia.org/wiki.

———. "Children as Mary, Joseph and a shepherd." 2007.

———. "Christmas Morning." 2007.

———. "Christmas Wreath."

———. "Family Reunion." 2007.

———. "Home Christmas Decorations." 2007.

———. "Lunar Phases." Created from NASA public domain images.

———. "Provo River at Canyon Glen."

———. "Provo Utah Temple near Squaw Peak."

———. "Rock Canyon."

———. "Santa putting gifts by a small Christmas tree."

———. "Santa Claus with my grandson."

———. "Scout Moral Compass."

———. "Wilderness Trail." Rock Canyon.

SWINDLE, Liz Lemon. http://www.foundationarts.com.

———. "The Holy Men." Used by permission.

———. "She Shall Bring Forth A Son." Used by permission.

———. "Silent Night." Used by permission.

ABOUT THE AUTHOR

Monte F. Shelley works at Brigham Young University in the Neal A. Maxwell Institute for Religious Scholarship. He is a member of the WordCruncher® software team that helps publish electronic texts such as the *Dead Sea Scrolls*, *Popol Vuh*, and *Joseph Smith Translation* (JST). He enjoys researching scripture related topics. He has served as a missionary, Scoutmaster, high councilor, bishop, branch president in the Missionary Training Center, and gospel doctrine teacher.

Monte and his wife, Elona K. Shelley, have six children and fourteen grandchildren.

We wish you a merry "Mary" Christmas!